Walking between the Times

Paul's Moral Reasoning

J. PAUL SAMPLEY

FORTRESS PRESS   Minneapolis

To all my students
(who taught me so much)
and to
Arlan F. Fuller, Jr.
Michael C. Sanders
William A. Shucart
William C. Wood
(who walk euschēmonōs)

From Sally and me

WALKING BETWEEN THE TIMES
Paul's Moral Reasoning

Copyright © 1991 Augsburg Fortress. All rights reserved. Except for brief quotations in critical articles or reviews, no part of this book may be reproduced in any manner without prior written permission from the publisher. Write to: Permissions, Augsburg Fortress, 426 S. Fifth St., Box 1209, Minneapolis, MN 55440.

All scripture quotations are the author's own translation except those noted as RSV, from the Revised Standard Version of the Bible, copyright © 1946, 1952, and 1971 by the Division of Christian Education of the National Council of Churches.

Interior and cover design: Publishers' WorkGroup
Cover art: Feather Sedam

Library of Congress Cataloging-in-Publication Data

Sampley, J. Paul.
    Walking between the times : Paul's moral reasoning / J. Paul
Sampley.
        p.   cm.
    Includes index.
    ISBN 0-8006-2479-3 (alk. paper)
    1. Paul the Apostle, Saint—Ethics.   2. Ethics in the Bible.
3. Bible. N.T. Epistles of Paul—Criticism, interpretation, etc.
I. Title.
BS2655.E8S25   1991
241'.092—dc20   90-26775
                                                          CIP

The paper used in this publication meets the minimum requirements of American National Standard for Information Sciences—Permanence of Paper for Printed Library Materials, ANSI Z329.48–1984.   ∞™

Manufactured in the U.S.A.   AF 1-2479

95   94   93   92   91   1   2   3   4   5   6   7   8   9   10

Contents

84622

Preface

Two times frame Paul's thought world or symbolic universe. One is the death and resurrection of Jesus Christ, which marks the origin of the new life of faith. The other is Christ's return, or Parousia, which will signal the culmination of God's purposes with the world. Paul is concerned with how believers behave, or walk, between these two times.

Two questions have fired much of my investigation of Paul in recent years: How did Paul do his moral reasoning and what resources did he think were available to those who were in Christ? Paul's letters are written conversations with various communities of believers across the northeast quadrant of the Mediterranean world. This book asks how Paul approaches moral issues. It focuses on Paul as his letters show him arriving at moral counsel or disclosing some already-established teaching about how his followers ought to behave. The study does not pursue the interesting questions of how well or how poorly Paul's different communities understood him or put his counsel into practice.

Unless otherwise noted, the translations of Paul's letters are mine. Paul's predilection for technical terms, for using words in such a way as to make them take on a special meaning, is the reason for occasional Greek transliterations in the text. I have tried to keep references to the Greek to a minimum so that there is not too much distraction, but have included them so that the curious student may see patterns in Paul's choice of terms.

Many people have favored me with a close reading of the manuscript and with suggestions. I appreciate their time and their sharing of themselves with me and with Sally in this effort. In particular I want to thank Wayne and Martha Meeks, each of whom made many helpful suggestions. One of my former students whom I count as friend, Feather Sedam, now an artist, read the manuscript and produced the illustration for the cover, a commentary on what I perceive to be the shape of Paul's moral reasoning.

Finally, the staff at Fortress Press continues to be supportive and helpful in ways that authors know and appreciate. I especially want to express my gratitude and fondness for John A. Hollar, who for decades was such a delight to work with. He knew I was working on this study for some years and inquired about it from time to time. I am pleased that it was he who accepted it for publication; I am profoundly saddened that he did not live to see it in print.

Boston University   J.P.S.
Boston, Massachusetts

Prologue

Ancient letters such as Paul's epistles can be fruitfully studied for what they disclose about the author's assumptions and understandings. As different as the recipients of Paul's correspondence are, and as distinct as their behavioral problems are, an identifiable person is the author—Paul, who stands foursquare in the middle of these letters. To receive the gospel is to receive Paul. To live as he does—to use Paul's metaphor—is to walk properly. Therefore, for Paul, God's gospel and "my gospel" are the same.

First, this book will establish a fuller and clearer picture of Paul's own thought world. With strong assistance from their social groups, people construct their own thought world or conceive reality so that being and doing make sense; then they behave with respect to that framework. This framework is adjusted as people observe what kinds of things or actions help them in this world. The apostle Paul came to understand that God had a hitherto undisclosed plan (Rom. 1:1-6; 3:21-22; 2 Cor. 1:20; cf. Rom. 16:25-26) that hinged on the death and resurrection of Jesus Christ and called for people to live their lives in accord with what God was doing. Paul had a fairly well-delineated picture of God's plan, of where people are within the framework of that plan, and of how people ought to live and behave between now and the imminent end of this age.

Second, this book will illuminate how Paul thought believers in God ought to live and behave and how Paul's distinctive thought world provides the context and the resources for his deliberations regarding appropriate behavior. We will not be concerned with how well the Philippians or the Corinthians understood Paul. Rather, our focus will remain upon what Paul's letters tell us about how he understood that believers should walk in the time remaining.

Third, this book aims to understand Paul's moral reasoning, that is, how Paul arrives at his counsels and convictions regarding proper behavior for believers, what he thinks that behavior is, and what resources he and all other believers have in such deliberations. I presume that no genuine understanding of Paul's moral reasoning can be gotten without seeing it consistently planted in the heart of Paul's symbolic universe. Additional issues will need clarification as we focus on how Paul thinks that believers ought to live and behave: Why does Paul conclude that such behavior is desirable? What resources does Paul have to assist in the determination of appropriate behavior? What resources does Paul think are available to his readers?

The book concludes with a few reflections on some issues on which modern readers may experience dissonance with Paul's thought world and with his moral reasoning. The Epilogue reviews the study and highlights some distinctive features of Paul's moral reflection.

Our sources in this study will be Paul's seven letters whose authenticity is, generally speaking, not disputed. Most scholars agree that Paul wrote Romans, 1 and 2 Corinthians, Galatians, Philippians, 1 Thessalonians, and Philemon. Methodologically it seems proper to ground the study upon those letters.

Among the Pauline letters, only Romans is written by Paul alone. All of the others claim joint authorship. For this study, which aims at a disclosure of Paul's thought world, coauthorship presents an interesting methodological problem. The problem, however, is put in perspective when it is recognized that Timothy, Paul's double, is the coauthor in four of the remaining six letters (2 Cor. 1:1; Phil. 1:1; 1 Thess. 1:1; Philemon 1). Is it likely in 1 Corinthians that "brother Sosthenes" is so different and distinct from Paul that he puts a radically different stamp on 1 Corinthians? I shall suppose that each of the seven letters presents a primary source for determining the scope and shape of Paul's thought world and moral reasoning.

This book is not an old-fashioned ethics text—if by that one means a study of Paul's consideration of various ethical issues. Nor is it a constructive ethics book in which parts of Paul's thinking are extrapolated to deal creatively with an issue of moment in modern times.

This study also is not intended to be a theology of Paul, even though Paul's theological reflections do ground his thought world. Scholars since Rudolf Bultmann agree that Paul's moral reflections cannot be separated from his theological understandings. The two are inextricable; to inquire of ethical matters in Paul's letters is to wrestle with theological issues, and vice versa.

At no point do Paul's letters offer detached, disinterested theological reflection; likewise, nowhere does Paul dispassionately analyze moral reasoning. Paul's moral reflection, so widespread in his letters, is always occasioned by a specific situation and is always couched in theological reflection as a part of Paul's thought world. Even Romans, as much as it may be shaped by Paul's situation, nevertheless tries to engage the Roman believers "rather boldly on some points" (15:15).

One final disclaimer is important: This book does not undertake a comprehensive treatment of all the features of Paul's thought world. It is not concerned, for example, with how justification fits in Paul's thought world, but rather with how the justified person is to discern what it means to walk properly before God.

PART ONE

PAUL'S FRAME OF REFERENCE

1

The Two Horizons of Paul's Thought World

The death and resurrection of Jesus Christ is the primary reference point in Paul's thought world. Paul sees past, present, and future in light of that pivotal event. For Paul, believers relate to the death and resurrection of Christ as the formative event in their past. Believers are the ones who "have died with Christ," "have been bought with a price," and "have been brought from death to life" (Rom. 6:13). They are the ones to whom faith came when Christ came, that is, when Christ was preached to them (Gal. 3:23-25). Having been set free from sin (Rom. 6:18), having died to sin (6:2), believers "have been united with him in a death like his" (6:5 RSV).

As these citations suggest, Paul relates to his followers as persons whose lives have been changed by the power of the gospel. They are people with a former life; they are no longer who they used to be. "Now" is balanced over against "no longer"; their "present" life is set in opposition to their "former" life.

Changed as the believers are, however, in Paul's view their present and future are not identical. Believers do not yet have access to the fullness of their inheritance. The Corinthians especially collapsed the future into the present, and Paul labored with them to distinguish what believers already have from what they have not yet been granted.

In Paul's view, believers' lives can be placed somewhere along the middle of a spectrum:

no longer	now/already	not yet

Shared death with Christ marks the beginning of the already-present life in Christ and the termination of the former, now no-longer life.

1. *No longer.* Paul, all of whose letters address believing communities, often refers to his recipients' pasts to explain or clarify their present circumstances and, in so doing, contrasts their former and present existences. "While we were yet weak," "while we were still sinners," and "while we were enemies" (Rom. 5:6, 8, 10), God's grace broke through and replaced enmity with peace, sin with faith, and helplessness with God's strength. He contrasts the Thessalonians' former worship of idols with their present service to "the living and true God" (1 Thess. 1:9); and he similarly counsels the Galatians:

> But, then, when you did not know God, you were enslaved to the ones who by nature are not gods. Now, though, knowing God, no, rather being known by God, how can you turn again to the weak and impoverished elemental spirits to whom you want to be enslaved again? (4:8-9)

2. *Now/Already.* Paul sees that believers are drawn from the present into the future that God is bringing. That future is a time whose glory is beyond compare (1 Cor. 15:42-44), a time when the entire creation "will be freed from slavery to deterioration unto the glorious freedom of God's children" (Rom. 8:21). The future is the time when the "new creation" (2 Cor. 5:17; Gal. 6:15) begun in Christ's death and resurrection will be completed, when God will be vindicated (1 Cor. 15:24-28), and when believers will "arrive at the resurrection from the dead" (Phil. 3:11). The not yet is the future horizon of Paul's thought world.

3. *Not Yet.* Believers are no longer to live as they formerly did. As rich as their new life in Christ is, however, believers live in anticipation of the fulfillment.

Yet Paul does not simply jettison the past. Abraham is used as the type of the faithful person (Romans 4; Galatians 3). "All the promises of God find their Yes in [Christ]" (2 Cor. 1:20 RSV). God's faithfulness and truthfulness are powerfully affirmed by Paul (Rom. 3:3-4; 15:8). "The gifts and the call of God are irrevocable" (Rom. 11:29 RSV), so the forebears of the Jews are beloved and elect because God has made a commitment to them. Those same forebears were "baptized into Moses" and "ate the same spiritual food and all drank the same spiritual drink" (1 Cor. 10:2-4) while they were led across the wilderness by God.

No Longer–Now/Already–Not Yet

In Christ's death and resurrection God broke the stranglehold of sin and freed all people everywhere to become a part of God's people and redemptive purpose. The law and the prophets have borne witness to God's righteousness (Rom. 3:21). The gospel was preached beforehand to Abraham (Gal. 3:8), but all the promises of God are now made good in Jesus Christ (2 Cor. 1:20; cf. Rom. 16:25-27). What the prophets anticipated is real and present in Christ Jesus for the believers: a foretaste and promise of all the good that God has in store for them.

These apocalyptic convictions are foundational to Paul's thought world. In his letters Paul consistently holds to his belief that God's apocalyptic triumph is at hand. Indeed in Christ's death and resurrection, God has broken sin's power and already has begun the new creation in the midst of the old world whose present form is passing away (1 Cor. 7:31). In this way the end impinges upon the present.

Paul's apocalyptic outlook may be distinguished from that of many of his contemporaries. Most apocalyptic writers looked at the oppression being meted out to them and acknowledged that the times were indeed evil. Through the vision or insight granted by God these apocalyptic seers declared that things were going to get worse for a (usually short) period. Then, after people had suffered more than it might seem they could bear, God would act decisively to destroy evil and its minions. The world, so encumbered with evil, would either be destroyed altogether or created anew; the same would be true for the heavens if they had been contaminated by evil (cf. Revelation 12). In such an apocalyptic construction, history and redemption are often opposed to one another. The world and human history are to be destroyed. The faithful are to be translated to a new heaven or a new earth. The seriousness with which apocalyptists view evil and its power requires the rejection of the past—and even present—and the installation in its place of a longing for God's redemptive power *beyond* history as we know it. One can diagram most apocalyptic views as follows:

cosmos under evil's power		new heaven, new earth
	JUDGMENT	
	END OF AGE	
old, present, aeon {ALREADY}		future aeon {NOT YET}

Paul shares with this general outlook the following understandings:
the present age or aeon is dominated by sin and evil;
hope rests not in tinkering with or adjusting the structures that exist but in God's ultimate triumph;
the faithful will suffer between now and the end;
the faithful must show patient endurance and steadfastness;
the end will involve a judgment and bring about a reversal by which those who have been oppressed will be vindicated against their enemies.

Paul's apocalyptic outlook differs from other such outlooks in significant ways. Although he expects a day of judgment when God will terminate this aeon or age, Paul is convinced that the new aeon has begun to break into the middle of the old aeon in a decisive way in Jesus Christ's death and resurrection. The new creation has begun (2 Cor. 5:17). The present form of this world is already passing away (1 Cor. 7:31). Paul expresses the same viewpoint in different terms when he talks about believers "discharging their obligations as citizens" in this world (politeuomai; Phil. 1:27) while enjoying contemporaneous citizenship in heaven (Phil. 3:20).

Christ's death and resurrection broke sin's domineering hold over human beings. In this event, God's redemptive purposes gained a beachhead. The same moment signalled the end of sin's power and the inauguration of the new age. But neither the end of sin nor the fullness of the new age is present completely. Sin has received a death blow, but it still stalks about, searching for a base of operations (cf. Rom. 7:8, 11). Similarly, the new creation has begun in the glorious freedom that God's children already enjoy and will receive its culmination when the rest of creation "will be set free from slavery to deterioration" (Rom. 8:21).

The apocalyptic vision that stands at the heart of Paul's gospel lacks the characteristic emphasis on two successive, separate ages. For Paul, beginning with Christ's death and resurrection, the two ages stand alongside one another until Christ's Parousia, judgment day. Accordingly, those who are in Christ—that is, those who have died with Christ—live in both worlds, in both ages, simultaneously. That is why, in the Lord's supper traditions, believers proclaim Christ's death until he comes (1 Cor. 11:26). The Lord's supper defines the context of Christian life, from the foundational sharing of Christ's death to its culmination in Christ's return at the end of history.

Until Christ comes in judgment, believers live in a world whose structures are passing away. However, they have been delivered from the clutches of sin and are assured that at the consummation they will be saved — they will be like Christ and will have a resurrection like his. Then death, sin's powerful arm, will not be able to reach them.

Paul's apocalyptic view can be diagrammed as follows:

old age   God's kingdom/glory

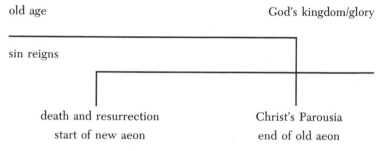

sin reigns

death and resurrection   Christ's Parousia
start of new aeon   end of old aeon

present form of this world passing
new creation is begun
believers already died with Christ
citizens of two worlds
confidently expect resurrection like Christ's

Now–No Longer: The Present
in Light of the Past

Believers are citizens of two worlds, living at once in the old and the new. Sin's power is broken and believers look forward with confidence to God's ultimate and full victory at Christ's Parousia. This apocalyptic vision is the frame of reference from which Paul's reflection and counsel arise. How do believers behave now, in the present? That is Paul's major concern; however, he sometimes describes the life appropriate to faith by contrasting it with believers' former manner of living. On such occasions, Paul's counsel takes the following form: Now this, no longer that. Whenever Paul employs these constructions, his interest in the past is solely for the light it sheds by contrast on the present. The movement of his remarks, however, always starts with the *now* and is subsequently directed toward the *no longer*.

Now in Christ

Paul thinks of believers' relationship with Christ in terms of solidarity with, participation in, or belonging to Christ. Except for rare, uncharacteristic remarks, Paul does not speak of Christ's death primarily as a sacrifice (Rom. 3:24). Neither does he think of Christ's death as a substitution made in place of the death that people might be said to deserve. Instead, Paul most frequently expresses believers' relationship to Christ as being "in Christ." Those who have faith are one together in Christ. This solidarity with Christ is Paul's primary identification of believers.

Even life apart from faith is conceived by Paul as a solidarity—a solidarity with Adam and his trespass. Sin came into the world through Adam "and death through sin" with the result that "death spread to all," not because of some genetic disposition to sin transmitted unfailingly from Adam onwards, but because all people sinned (Rom. 5:12). All people became like Adam precisely by sinning. Solidarity with Adam in sin was, however, a forerunner (typos) of the new solidarity now offered in Christ (Rom. 5:14).

Paul surveys two rival solidarities that represent two different ways of living: one in accord with Adam and his sin with its attendant death; the other in Christ with its free gift of righteousness and promise of eternal life (Rom. 5:17, 21). Until Christ's Parousia, the consummation of God's purposes in and with the world, these two ways of living stand as fundamental but incompatible human options: the one attainable through any human being's sin, the other only through God's gracious gift.

Life Prior to Faith

From the Pauline corpus one can put together a picture of Paul's view of life prior to or apart from faith: a life of wrongful relation to God, a life of enslavement to sin, and, at its worst, a life of immorality (porneia; 1 Cor. 5:1; 6:18). The people who live this life, the "unrighteous" as he calls them (1 Cor. 6:9), "shall not inherit God's kingdom" (6:9-10).

Paul sees the old aeon, the old age, from the perspective of the new aeon. He looks back from the life of faith through the prism provided by Christ's death and resurrection and sees a study in contrasts. The new age, or the new creation, began with Christ's death and resurrection (2 Cor. 5:17; cf. Gal. 6:15). In Christ's death believers were reconciled to God. Paul also expresses this conviction by a juristic concept: believers were justified by God (Rom. 5:9-10). Believers became righteous. Faith, that right relationship of trusting dependence upon God, became possible by God's grace, by God's freely bestowed, unmerited gift (Romans 4). Enmity toward God is ended; believers now have peace with God (Rom. 5:1).

The old aeon—marked by enmity toward and alienation from God (Rom. 5:6)—is characterized by a fundamental confusion about the proper relationship between creature and creator (Rom. 1:19-28). Paul's code word for this alienation or brokenness is sin. Paul does not write much of sins. Rather, he thinks of sin as if it were a power stalking about looking for a beachhead (cf. Rom. 7:8, 11) from which to launch a campaign to take control over someone's life. Sin leads to death—that is axiomatic for Paul (Rom. 6:16, 21). Sin pays off in death (6:23). So the old age is the aeon of sin, the aeon of death. Its grip is strong and firm.

In Paul's thought world, only God's grace breaks the power of sin and grants freedom, redeeming a sinner from continued slavery to sin. Whenever sin establishes its power over a person, that person is robbed of the freedom and self-determination that would allow an escape. Those under sin are free only to sin; they cannot simply will to become righteous. That is what Paul means when he writes to the Romans, "When you were slaves of sin, you were free with respect to righteousness" (6:20).

In Paul's view, sin is not simply individualistic malfeasance. Romans 1:22-27 makes clear that human sinfulness has disrupted and harmed not just individual sinners, but also the created order. Later in the same letter, as Paul ponders God's ultimate redemptive purposes, he writes that the whole creation is waiting for redemption "from its bondage to deterioration" (8:19-22).

The Two Aeons Coexist

The aeon of sin and death continues to exist, according to Paul, alongside the new aeon of life and righteousness. The old age will come to its conclusion with the Parousia of Christ. Throughout the letters of Paul we see that he expected the end of the age in the near future. Even in Romans, his last surviving letter, he declares: "For salvation is now nearer to us than when we first believed; the night is far gone, the day is near" (13:11-12). The "day," the "Day of the Lord," and the "Parousia of Christ" all refer to the anticipated consummation of God's dealing with the world and with the old aeon. At that time death, the last enemy, and with it, sin, will be defeated (1 Cor. 15:54-57).

Until the consummation, God deals with both ages and their adherents simultaneously. The people who belong to the old age — the ones under sin's power — are "the perishing ones" (1 Cor. 1:18; 2 Cor. 2:15; cf. Phil. 1:28; 1 Thess. 2:13-16) who are subject to God's wrath and severity (Rom. 11:22). The people who are in Christ, the believers, are recipients of God's kindness (Rom. 11:22); they are the ones who are "being saved" (1 Cor. 1:18; Phil. 1:28) and who live in the new age.

Those who are in Christ must expect animosity and opposition from those who are perishing. Such opposition is part of the distress that engages the whole cosmos during the last times. Far from escaping this distress, believers are assured of experiencing it. Paul reminds the Thessalonians that he had alerted them to this prospect; when he receives word that they are experiencing opposition he takes it as a sign that they are living properly (1 Thess. 3:3). He writes to the Corinthians that things could not be going better for him in Ephesus. His evidence? He has a wide door open to him and there are abundant opponents (1 Cor. 16:9). Adversaries should not frighten believers; opponents are concomitant with the tension between the two ages (Phil. 1:28). Paul even hints that those who try to live properly have always been somewhat at odds with the rest of the population (Gal. 4:29).

Believers are transformed people. They no longer relate to the world in the way they did before God's grace entered their lives. They used to conform to the norms of the old aeon; now conformity to the new age is expected of them. Living according to the new aeon would be easier if the old aeon had disappeared, but of course in Paul's view it has not. The old aeon, under sin's dominion, tries to lure believers to return to it. Paul warns the Romans about slipping and conforming once again to the old age (Rom. 12:2). He urges the Philippians to be "faultless and uncrooked, God's children without blemish in the midst of an unscrupulous and depraved generation, among whom you shine as lights in the world" (2:15).

Paul does not urge believers to flee the world; they are to live the new life, the new creation, in the midst of this age that is headed for its condemnation (1 Cor. 11:32). Believers should thrive in the face of opposition. Therefore, Paul says he lives and does his ministry in the world but does not fight according to the world's terms or with the power of the world (2 Cor. 10:3). This world has its own rulers, its own wisdom, its own spirit (1 Cor. 2:6, 12). Once, even though Paul knows that there is no other God (1 Cor. 8:4; Rom. 3:30), he even mentions "the god of this aeon" who "has blinded the minds of the unfaithful" (2 Cor. 4:4). Believers serve under a different Lord, have their own wisdom, and have been granted a different Spirit.

Accordingly, there are two ways to walk—the metaphor Paul likes to use for living one's life: one can walk according to human standards (1 Cor. 3:3), that is, in the old age or world. Alternatively, one can walk or conduct one's life according to the Holy Spirit (Gal. 5:25). Paul is concerned that believers may slip back to their old behavior (Rom. 12:2).

Paul believes that the world has been crucified to him and he to the world (Gal. 6:14) and thus the cross represents for Paul the actual shattering of the old aeon's power over believers. It is a two-way break: the world's power over Paul is broken and Paul's attachment to the world is severed. The cross therefore provides double insulation against the world's control and allure for all who are in Christ. That is why believers are free to live the new life in the midst of the old aeon.

Paul used popular Cynic and Stoic views of life to describe how believers, whose commonwealth is in heaven (Phil. 3:20), can live in this world even as it is passing away. They are to live "as if not" (*hōs mē*) having involvement in it:

> The time is shortened; for the remainder, the ones who have wives as if not having them, and the ones weeping as if not weeping, and the ones rejoicing as if not rejoicing, and the ones purchasing as if not possessing, and the ones using the world as if not making full use: for the present form of this world is passing away. (1 Cor. 7:29-31)

Paul practices what he preaches, and hopes his readers will as well:

> We are treated as impostors, and yet are true; as unknown, and yet well known; as dying, and behold we live; as punished, and yet not killed; as sorrowful, yet always rejoicing; as poor, yet making many rich; as having nothing, and yet possessing everything. (2 Cor. 6:8-10 RSV)

Because the old world is passing away, sin and the structures through which it used to operate no longer dictate the lives of the believers and they are free to walk in a different way while still in the old world. They remain subject to the world's sorrows and poverty, but their symbolic universe has undergone radical transformation. Whereas their legitimization formerly came from others and the opinions of others guided their actions, now believers are secure in Christ; they know they are accepted by God and therefore are freed from the world's clutches.

Saying that Christ died for all people (2 Cor. 5:14-15) means that Christ's death is God's grace presented as a call to each individual, as an occasion for that individual to trust God and be freed from the power of sin. In Christ's death God's call goes out to people: "And he died in behalf of all people so that the ones who live might no longer live for themselves . . ." (2 Cor. 5:15). Why does this verse first say that Christ "died for all" and then mention, not "all," but "the ones who live"? Christ's death is all-inclusive, "for all"; "the ones who live" is a smaller group from among the "all" for whom Christ died. Paul knows from experience that not all people respond to God's grace and begin to live in Christ. But Christ died for all people, even for those who do not respond positively.

Paul declares that after Christ's death and resurrection — "from now on, therefore" — the believers' perspective on people is radically altered, whether or not others have responded affirmatively to the call. "We, ourselves, regard no one" as we used to, namely, according to the ways of the world (*kata sarka;* 2 Cor. 5:16). Paul does not say that believers regard no other believers as they did before; he says that "we regard no one" as before, whether they have become believers or not. Paul declares that believers are transformed not only in their new life of faith but also in their entire view of the world and of all people. Christ's death and resurrection has become for Paul the basis for living with and being among God's creatures. Paul and all other believers must now respond to all people as ones for whom Christ has died. That death makes them special whether or not they have responded in faith. Christ's death and resurrection therefore determine not only how a believer walks or behaves in the world but also how the believer understands his or her relation to the world and to all other people in the cosmos.

The whole world is going to be held accountable to God (Rom. 3:19). All people will be judged on the basis of what they have done while they have had the gift of life. People who live improperly receive God's judgment (Rom. 1:24-25, 32; 2:5, 8). Those who live appropriately will be rewarded: there will be "glory and honor and peace for every one who works the good" (Rom. 2:10).

The Contrast between Present and Past

Paul's "now–no longer" references function in four ways. First, they heighten the believers' awareness of the changes that have taken place in their lives. The new life of faith is confirmed and defined by its differences from the past. Second, the transformation in believers' lives is credited to God's power, that is, to the power of the gospel. The differences therefore heighten believers' awareness of God's grace at work in the transformation. Assertions such as "we are now justified" and "while we were enemies we were reconciled" (Rom. 5:9-10 RSV), by their passive construction, make clear that believers did not justify themselves or bring about their own reconciliation. The understood, but unstated, agent in such Pauline passive constructions is God.

Third, Paul's contrasts function as instruction concerning how to walk, that is, how to live the life appropriate to faith. That life is portrayed in part by contrasting it with the way Paul's followers walked before faith came to them. Paul has nothing of the museum curator's interest in the believers' pasts; his is the preacher's preoccupation with heightening his readers' understanding of their present.

Finally, Paul contrasts the present and past to heighten his followers' understanding of God. The life of faith, as Paul understands it, is not a realignment or rearrangement of features of one's prefaith life. Rather, the life of faith is part of the new creation, created by God out of nothing. Paul uses the typology of Abraham in Romans 4 to disclose that the God with whom people deal is the God who brings life out of death and who brings things into existence (4:17). The life of faith is a new thing brought into existence by the God of Abraham and of Jesus Christ. It contrasts starkly with life before faith: "dead to sin . . . alive to God" (Rom. 6:11), "slaves of sin . . . slaves of righteousness" (Rom. 6:17-18), and "no longer a slave but a son" (Gal. 4:7).

Already–Not Yet: The Future in Light of the Present

Paul's understanding of the relationship between present and future is more complex than his view of the relationship between present and past. We learn of Paul's teachings regarding the Lord's supper in his response to the Corinthians' trivialization of it. Paul is moved to rehearse the Lord's supper traditions, and in that recounting we are granted an insight not only into the history of those traditions in the early church but also into Paul's fundamental frame of reference. "For as often as you eat this bread and drink the cup, you proclaim the death of the Lord until he comes" (1 Cor. 11:26). In Paul's thought world, the Lord's supper marks the boundaries within which believers live: from Christ's death until his Parousia. Christ's death — and the believer's sharing it with Christ — delineates the beginning of faith. Christ's return, which for Paul also signals the end of history and the consummation of God's purposes for the cosmos, is the ultimate boundary of faith. So to Paul, the keeping of the Lord's supper serves as a reminder, with each observation, of the borders between which all believers live.

Paul is a perspectival thinker, that is, he is able to look at a particular matter from more than one standpoint. For example, Paul refers to Epaphroditus, the Philippians' emissary to Paul, as "my brother and fellow worker and fellow soldier" and in the same sentence depicts him as the Philippians might view him: "your messenger and servant to my need" (Phil. 2:25). Similarly, Onesimus, the runaway slave mentioned in the Letter to Philemon, is a slave in the world's view but is a brother in Christ when considered from the standpoint of faith.

Paul also employs his perspectival thinking on a crucial christological point. From one perspective, Paul thinks of Christ's death and resurrection as a completed, past event. In this perspective, Christ's death and resurrection are so fundamentally interlinked that the mention of the one seems to assume the other. However, when Paul considers Christ's death and resurrection from the standpoint of the believers' participation in them, then he construes the matter quite differently, sharply and consistently distinguishing between believers' already sharing Christ's death and their not yet attaining a resurrection like Christ's. So Christ has died and been raised but, prior to the Parousia, believers only share in Christ's death. One of the clearest places to see this is in Philippians. Paul, viewing himself as the model, describes his own status in the life of faith. Paul writes of his desire to know Christ "and the power of his resurrection . . . that somehow I should arrive unto the resurrection from the dead" (Phil. 3:10-11). Verse 12 makes it clear that Paul knows he has not yet been raised with Christ: "Not that I have already received or am already perfect; but I pursue to seize it" (3:12). This perspectival separation of believers' already-shared death with Christ and their not-yet-attained resurrection is present throughout Paul's letters. Paul affirms to the Romans that sharing Christ's death assures them of a future participation in the resurrection:

> We were buried therefore with him by baptism into death, so that as Christ was raised from the dead by the glory of the Father, we too might walk in newness of life. For if we have been united with him in a death like his, we shall certainly be united with him in a resurrection like his. (6:4-5 RSV)

Believers have died with Christ and, though they do not yet have a resurrection like his, they do "walk in newness of life."

At least some of the Corinthians failed to understand that the resurrection as Paul understood it was a future expectation, and so he subjects them to his blistering irony: "Already you are satiated! Already you have become rich! Apart from us you have reigned! O that you did reign, so that we might reign along with you!" (1 Cor. 4:8). Too bad that apostles do not have it so good, he continues (4:9-13). To these same confused Corinthians Paul later pointedly notes that though Christ has already died and been raised from the dead, Christ is "the first fruits of the ones who are sleeping" (1 Cor. 15:20). The other believers "shall all be made alive, *but each in his own turn:* Christ the first fruits, then the ones belonging to Christ at his coming" (*parousia;* 1 Cor. 15:22-23, emphasis added). Here Paul draws on his Jewish heritage and refers to Christ as the "first fruits," as the offering that sanctifies and insures the rest of the harvest (cf. Exod. 34:22; Lev. 23:15-22; Num. 28:26; Deut. 16:9-12). Believers have already experienced death with Christ and they will share in a resurrection like Christ's at his Parousia, when God's purposes for and with the cosmos will be consummated.

We can see Paul's frame of reference as he views life in the now–not yet mode of reflection. The "now" for the believers rests in their being in Christ, in their life of faith. Participation in Christ's death is the beginning of the believers' faith journey. The journey is not concluded until, by God's decisive and vindicating action, Christ comes, at which time history as the believers have known it comes to an end. So the now and the not yet frame the present and future life of the believers.

When Paul thinks about the relation between the now and the not yet in the life of faith, he most often thinks in terms of continuity, of how the one leads toward the other. He encourages believers to build from the now to the not yet with the assistance of God's ongoing grace. However, when Paul shifts his perspective and ponders the glory and grandeur of what God will do in the future, he considers the present not even worthy of comparison with the glory that God has in store for the believers. In this mode of reflection, continuity gives way to contrast.

Continuity and Contrast

Most of Paul's employment of the now–not yet constructions affirms a solid link between present and future in the life of faith. As we have seen, for Paul the future reaches its culmination in Christ's Parousia. Paul pictures the end time in a variety of ways: maturity, salvation, and the Day of the Lord. Each one has its counterpart in the present.

Paul sees the end time as one where the believers, having grown steadily from the time of their rebirth, arrive at maturity or, as the term is sometimes translated, perfection (*teleios;* Phil. 3:12). He chides the Corinthians for being like babies, though they ought to have grown up sufficiently to handle more than baby food (1 Cor. 3:1-2). Onesimus has become Paul's child in the faith (Philemon 10). New believers are God's children (Rom. 8:16) who profess their new birth by crying "Abba, Father" (Rom. 8:15; Gal. 4:6).

Paul also describes God's end-time accomplishment as salvation. Those who are reconciled to God, that is, those who are justified (Rom. 5:6-10), are assured of salvation: they shall be saved (Rom. 5:9-10). Believers are the ones who are being saved (1 Cor. 1:18; Phil. 1:28). Salvation is a goal toward which believers are supposed to work — "with fear and trembling, work out your own salvation" (Phil. 2:12) — because God is at work in them (Phil. 2:13; cf. Eph. 2:5, 8). For Paul, salvation and hope are firmly linked (1 Thess. 5:8).

The "Day of the Lord" (1 Cor. 1:8; Phil. 1:6, 10; 1 Thess. 5:2), or simply the "Day" (Rom. 2:16; 1 Cor. 3:13), is another way Paul envisions the end of this aeon. Connected with this image are judgment (Rom. 2:16; 14:10-12; 1 Cor. 4:5) and sharing a resurrection like Christ's (Phil. 3:10). One's fate at the judgment is linked directly to one's actions in the days before the Day (2 Cor. 5:10).

Strong christological links also reinforce the continuity between present and future in the life of the believers. Having died with Christ frees one from sin, but also means that one is now "in Christ." In Christ's resurrection from the dead the believers, that is, those who are in Christ, are assured that Christ is the "firstborn among many brothers" (Rom. 8:29); he is the "first fruits of the ones who are sleeping" (1 Cor. 15:20). The rest of the brothers and sisters, the remainder of the harvest, will be claimed at his Parousia (1 Cor. 15:23). Belonging to Christ, therefore, assures a direct link to God's consummation of history at the end time.

Paul's understanding of the manifold functions of the Holy Spirit also reassures believers of the continuity of their lives in the present with God's ultimate and future purposes. In a number of ways, the Holy Spirit is a prime eschatological link between the now and the not yet.

The Holy Spirit inaugurates the life of faith when it "bears witness with our spirit that we are God's children" (Rom. 8:16) and believers then call upon God as children (Rom. 8:15; Gal. 4:6). Paul's logic, manifest in his argument in Romans, follows the implications of this new status as God's children: "and if children, also heirs, heirs of God and co-heirs with Christ" (Rom. 8:17). The work of the Spirit at the inception of the life of faith has consequences for believers who will share the inheritance.

Paul makes a similar point when he refers to the Holy Spirit as a down payment or earnest money payment (*arrabōn*) given to believers by God. God "has sealed us and gives the down payment of the Spirit into our hearts" (2 Cor. 1:22; cf. 2 Cor. 5:5). The term translated "down payment" was a common legal and commercial term in Paul's time, actually a Semitic loanword. The first installment obligated the payer to make the rest of the payments. Paul uses strong language, therefore, in claiming that God's gift of the Holy Spirit to believers is the down payment on all that God will ultimately give them.

The gifts of the Spirit (*charismata*) that are given to the believers (Rom. 12:6-8; 1 Cor. 12:4-11), as well as the "fruit of the Spirit" (Gal. 5:22-23), are midcourse signs of God's continued presence and God's ultimate promise to make good on the down payment that the Spirit represents in the lives of the believers.

With these metaphors for the life of faith—childhood to maturity, down payment to full purchase, adoption to full share of the inheritance—it is clear that Paul views life in Christ as a process subject to growth or improvement. The Corinthians should be more mature (1 Cor. 3:1-2; 2 Cor. 6:13). Paul hopes for the Philippians' "advancement and joy in the faith" (Phil. 1:25) and appeals to the Thessalonians, who are doing well, to "do so more and more" (1 Thess. 4:1, 10 RSV). It can be of no surprise that he exalts communal "edification" and "encouragement" (1 Cor. 14:3). Many of Paul's images for the church emphasize increasing maturity or improvement: body (1 Cor. 12:12-26) and building and field (1 Cor. 3:9), for example.

Paul's reflections on the relationship between present and future largely focus on ways in which the present leads into the future. Theologically, Paul sees that what God has begun in Christ and in those who are in Christ will be consummated by God. Those who have died with Christ can be confident that, despite their suffering and hardships in the meantime, they will share in the glory that God will bring to fruition at Christ's Parousia. Therefore, believers are not without hope even though the opposition from the old aeon and its adherents is great. Paul insists that the continuity of God's actions begun in Christ's death and resurrection and to be completed in the Day of the Lord provides the basis for confidence with regard to both the present and the future.

Just as sin held its dependents firmly in its throes—and therefore brought continuity to the life of sin—so, by the power of God in Christ, the Holy Spirit, and the community of the faithful, believers can expect to have a life of continuity that stretches from their shared death with Christ to an expected resurrection like his at the end of the age.

Functions of Already–Not Yet

Paul's emphasis on continuity serves a number of purposes. First, the references to the future help believers to keep the present in perspective. For the Corinthian enthusiasts, for example, he was able to make clear just how much of the new life they had and how much they had yet to be granted. Second, pointing toward the future suggests to the readers that the present and what they have already in their grasp is not the whole of the story; to be an adopted baby is not yet to have in hand the entire glorious inheritance. Third, it provides a framework within which Paul can not only press for improvement and growth but also link divine initiative and human responsibility. It is God's grace that has made the origin of faith possible; it is God's kingdom that is going to be established at Christ's Parousia; and it will be God or Christ who will judge the hearts of people as well as what they have done while in the body (2 Cor. 5:10). On the side of human responsibility, Paul's already–not yet configuration enables him to construe the gift of faith as a stewardship that, because it is supposed to manifest itself in works of love, will encompass the entire life of the believer, from the inception of faith until the end-time judgment of the works that one has done.

Although Paul most often stresses the continuity between the believers' now and their not yet, he sometimes sees the two in tension. Paul knows that as great as the present is in Christ, with its new life and transformations, it pales in significance as Paul contemplates his vision of what is yet to come. Sometimes this contrast is cast in the "how much more" form. Twice in Rom. 5:6-11 Paul sees the believers' future salvation as beyond comparison with their present justification and reconciliation (5:9-10).

When in Romans 8 the present sufferings are seen in light of the future glory that God is about to reveal, there is no comparison because the latter so outshines the former (8:18). Paul is guided by an expected "eternal weight of glory beyond all measure and proportion"; he reckons, not from the visible, transient things, but from the unseen, eternal things (2 Cor. 4:17-18). His vision of the last times is one in which "what is mortal" is "swallowed up by life" (2 Cor. 5:4). As he explains to the Corinthians, some of whom have collapsed future glory and freedom into the present, the resurrection life in the end time will be a life in the body just as in the present (so there is indeed some continuity), but the resurrection body is like a seed: "It is sown in dishonor, it is raised in glory. It is sown in weakness, it is raised in power" (1 Cor. 15:43 RSV).

The continuity and contrast between present and future in the life of faith ground human action in history. Present events and human relationships are the context in which God's grace is made present and real and in which people must find ways to maximize their expressions of faithfulness and their works of love. What people do in the present is of primary importance to Paul because what they do while in the body will be that for which they are held accountable in the judgment.

Paul's frame of reference neither requires nor has as an ultimate concern escape from this world (as even Phil. 1:22-26 shows). Rather, for Paul the issue becomes how one lives in this world between the time of faith's beginning and Christ's Parousia.

2

Paul's Vista of Life in the World

We can reconstruct some of Paul's understanding of how things happen in the world, how power works, and how people operate. While his primary attention was focused on life within the community of believers, he was aware that these communities existed within larger social, economic, and political networks.

The Larger Context

Authorities and the Law

By the time Paul wrote 2 Corinthians 10–13, he had been the object of punishment three times by the Romans (2 Cor. 11:25; cf. Rom. 8:33) and five times by the Jews (2 Cor. 11:24; cf. 1 Thess. 2:15-16). Once, a governor employed a manhunt in Damascus to capture Paul, but Paul outwitted him (2 Cor. 11:32-33). He was incarcerated on several occasions (2 Cor. 6:5; 11:23; Philemon 1).

Paul also knew the failure of the law and its protection. Mobs stoned him (2 Cor. 11:25), and robbers attacked him (11:26). Travel was often precarious (11:26).

Sharing a widespread skepticism of legal structures, Paul viewed contemporary jurists as contemptible (1 Cor. 6:4) and did not expect good judgments and justice from the courts (1 Cor. 6:3-8).

For Paul, the rulers of this aeon are "doomed to perish" (1 Cor. 2:6; 15:24). They did not understand what was under way: "if they had known, they would not have crucified the Lord of glory" (1 Cor. 2:8). By crucifying the Lord of glory they unwittingly precipitated their own end. As part of this present, evil aeon, the rulers stand under the same eschatological judgment as sin and its manifestations: in Christ's death, God's judgment has been levied against the present aeon and its representatives; in Christ's resurrection, believers are promised God's ultimate vindication and their participation in the resurrection. The rulers still hold sway over this aeon, but they are doomed to pass away. Until God's vindication, however, authorities have power and must be dealt with seriously. Believers are to deal with governing authorities eschatologically, that is, knowing that the final power resides with God, but seeing the present as the arena in which life must be lived.

Given this, Paul's relatively positive words in Romans about authorities may be surprising until their context is clarified: prior to Rom. 13:1-7 Paul argues, by means of maxims, that people should live peaceably whenever possible (12:18), that vengeance must be left to God, that amicable treatment of enemies is the goal, and that evil must be overcome in the good (12:19-21). In Rom. 13:1-7 Paul, employing traditional materials (cf. 1 Pet. 2:13-17, Titus 3:1), pragmatically addresses the situation in Rome and encourages his readers to live in such a fashion that they not only do not draw the ire of authorities, but even receive the authorities' commendation (13:3). Paul may still be convinced, as he was when he wrote 1 Corinthians, that the authorities are doomed to pass away, but he breathes not a word of it in Romans.

Living in the World

Paul's use of the term *kosmos* shows various aspects of his thought world. The *kosmos* is the place of known habitation, perhaps the empire. That seems to be his view when he gives thanks to God that the Romans' "faith is proclaimed the whole world over" (Rom. 1:8). There was a time when God created this world (Rom. 1:20); so there will be a time when God will judge it and hold it accountable (Rom. 3:6, 19). The world is populated by evil people (1 Cor. 5:10) so numerous that believers cannot avoid them. No matter how enslaved the world is, Paul knows it is the place one lives and toward which one must figure out how to behave (2 Cor. 1:12). The world has a wisdom (1 Cor. 1:20; 3:19), a spirit (1 Cor. 2:12), power (1 Cor. 3:22), and concerns (1 Cor. 7:33-34) that are different from those of believers. The world needs to be and is being reconciled to God (2 Cor. 5:19) even though hostile elements still pervade it (Gal. 4:3, 9). Though it is "in slavery to decay" (Rom. 8:21), the creation longs to "obtain the glorious liberty of the children of God" (Rom. 8:21 RSV).

Insofar as the world continues to tempt believers to live at enmity with God, they must distinguish themselves from the evil that characterizes the world or they too will be condemned (1 Cor. 11:32). In fact, Paul considers believers to be "light-giving bodies," like stars, in the world (Phil. 2:15; cf. Matt. 5:14).

Cosmic powers and forces, although they are not deities (1 Cor. 8:5) and are actually weak and miserable, in some sense had once enslaved those who are now believers and would enslave them again if the believers were to succumb to them (Gal. 4:8-9). With their renewed wills and minds, however, believers control whether they will remain faithful or be led into subservience to one of these lesser powers.

There are demons and there is a tempter, Satan. Believers, however, are beyond the power of such creatures — unless they yield to temptation (1 Thess. 3:5; 1 Cor. 7:5). Satan indeed is on the prowl and lures people wherever and whenever possible. Satan has a plot to outwit the believers (2 Cor. 2:11), but they know what it is, so they should be forearmed. Satan masquerades as an "angel of light" and has minions who do the same; like people, however, their end will be in accord with their works (2 Cor. 11:14-15). Thus, Paul readily identified the opposition he experienced in Thessalonica as the work of Satan, and continued resistance there meant that Satan had prevented Paul from going to Thessalonica (1 Thess. 2:18).

Satan never functions in Paul's letters as a scapegoat for believers' missteps. Rather, references to Satan warn believers not to be seduced into Satan's grasp, not to return to their former servitude to sin. Human responsibility and, in cases of moral failure, human culpability are cornerstones in Paul's thought world. Individuals must take responsibility for their decisions and their actions.

Faithful people walk differently. They live by different standards and according to different norms. As a result, they experience rejection by those associated with the world and attacks, opposition, and slander are directed toward them (1 Cor. 4:12-13; 2 Cor. 4:7-11).

The world is a hazardous place. Transit by ship is perilous; wilderness areas and even rivers can be treacherous (2 Cor. 11:25-26). The weather does not always cooperate (2 Cor. 11:27). People do not always make the world easier. Robbers abound (2 Cor. 11:26; 1 Cor. 6:10). People revile and slander (1 Cor. 4:12-13); they murder; they gossip and make up stories designed to harm (Rom. 1:29-31). They are drunkards and they commit adultery (1 Cor. 6:9-10). They engage in sorcery (Gal. 5:20). They fawn over others and try to please them (1 Thess. 2:4-6). Some take advantage of others by living off of their goods (2 Cor. 11:9; 12:13).

Despite Paul's pessimism about the state of the world, however, he never is tempted by the gnostic notion that the world itself is evil. God created the world. God will redeem it, in fact, has already begun to do so. Paul's rich, world-affirming Jewish heritage is evident when, discussing what a believer can eat, he declares that faithful people can eat whatever is sold in the meat market. He comes to such clarity of judgment by hearing the scripture, "because the earth is the Lord's and the fullness of it" (1 Cor. 10:26; Ps. 24:1). Believers are Abraham's offspring and therefore are subject to the promise God made that Abraham and his descendants would inherit the world (Rom. 4:13).

A sense of belonging, often expressed in claims of citizenship, was important in Paul's time. He accommodates that desire by claiming that believers' commonwealth (*politeuma*) is not in this world but in heaven (Phil. 3:20). Such a declaration of otherworldly citizenship could have spawned an escapist mentality of detachment and noninvolvement in the world. Paul, however, expects his followers to remain involved in the world just as he has (Phil. 1:25): "Only discharge your obligations as citizens [*politeuomai*] worthy of the gospel of Christ" (Phil. 1:27). Though one's commonwealth is elsewhere, citizenship is exercised in this world despite one's dissonance with the world and those who live according to it.

Possessions

In Paul's letters we gain glimpses of his attitude toward possessions. He admits that at times he has had more and at other times less (Phil. 4:12), but neither extreme is of concern to him. He works with his hands enough to avoid being a burden to his followers (1 Thess. 2:9; 1 Cor. 4:12; 2 Cor. 12:13). Paul thought that as an apostle he deserved or had a right to support by his churches (Gal. 6:6; 1 Cor. 9:4, 6), but he was free not to enforce it.

Cynics had a long-standing tradition about possessions that is reflected in the following statement: "All things belong to the gods; the wise are friends of the gods; friends have things in common" (*Diogenes Laertius* 6.37). Paul's thought world is slightly different from that of the Cynics. Believers "possess everything" (2 Cor. 6:10) because they belong to Christ, who belongs to God (1 Cor. 3:23): "for all things are yours" (1 Cor. 3:21). God, who is the creator of all things will give all things to the believers with Christ (Rom. 8:32). In fact, whatever the believers now have is gracefully bestowed upon them by God and is therefore not a basis for bragging (1 Cor. 4:7).

Believers' relationship to possessions is analogous to their relationship to authorities. Just as there are authorities in the world with whom one must come to terms without granting them power at the center of one's life, so there are possessions and goods in the world that one can deal with, use, and even enjoy as long as one's involvement with them is an eschatological engagement. That is, the believer must realize that all things belong to the Creator and ultimately are subject to God's power. Then "those making purchases" can relate to the objects "as if not taking them into their possession" (1 Cor. 7:30). Believers can live as "those having nothing yet possessing everything" (2 Cor. 6:10). Because possessions and things are divested of power, having them grants no special status or prestige; lacking them is equally meaningless. Moreover, Paul is convinced that God will take care of those who trust God: "My God will supply your every need in accordance with his riches in glory in Christ Jesus" (Phil. 4:19; cf. Rom. 11:33).

Outsiders to the Faith

Paul knows that many people live as "enemies of the cross of Christ . . . their god is the belly and . . . they dote on earthly things" and "their end is annihilation" (Phil. 3:18-19). They are focused on immorality (*porneia*). There are so many such people that believers simply cannot avoid contact with them short of "exiting the world" (1 Cor. 5:10).

Sometimes the contact between believers and unbelievers is benign; sometimes it is positive for the outsiders (1 Cor. 7:12-16). Even at Thessalonica, where Paul and his followers are met with violent rejection, he nevertheless shows a vital concern for the unbelievers and urges believers to "walk becomingly to those outside" (1 Thess. 4:12; cf. Rom. 13:13; 1 Cor. 14:40). Even in the worst of situations, Paul seems to retain the hope that outsiders may be attracted to faith as they see it lived.

Paul relates flexibly to those outside the faith. At Corinth, the boundaries of the community are much more open, perhaps because Corinthian Christians have not experienced violent opposition from their compatriots. Corinthian believers are married to unbelievers and Paul does not counsel divorce unless the believer requests it (1 Cor. 7:15). Should unbelievers invite believers to dinner, Paul sees no problem with accepting such invitations (1 Cor. 10:27-30). Unbelievers have free access to Corinthian worship services, and Paul thinks that believers ought to conduct themselves and their services in such a way that nothing inhibits the gospel's impact on such outsiders (1 Cor. 14:21-25).

Even though unbelievers live as "enemies of the cross," they are nevertheless persons for whom Christ died. Because Christ died for all people (2 Cor. 5:14-15), Paul can never again view them as he used to (2 Cor. 5:16). They are valuable creatures because Christ values them.

The Household of Faith

While not forgetting those outside the faith, Paul pictures believers as having a special bond among themselves: "So, then, as we have the occasion, let us do good to all, but especially to those who belong to the household of faith" (Gal. 6:10). This sequence usually begins with the faithful and then extends beyond: "May the Lord cause you to increase and overflow in love to one another and to all, just as has happened from us to you" (1 Thess. 3:12). As love abounds "to one another" within the community of believers, so may it overflow to all people.

This common Pauline linking of believers and unbelievers occurs again in 1 Thess. 5:15: "See that you do not give someone back wrong for wrong, but always pursue good for one another and for all." By the time Paul writes to the Romans he has distilled this counsel into a maxim by which he hopes that Roman believers may be guided: "If possible, in matters under your control, live peacefully with all" (12:18).

Believers are not protected from suffering and difficulties. Christ is no barrier against problems. Being in Christ, believers share

Christ's sufferings (2 Cor. 1:5; Rom. 8:17). They are persecuted, opposed, and subjected to afflictions. As the creation experiences the birth pangs of its renewal, so the believers are partakers in the eschatological afflictions. The Thessalonians, for instance, experience great opposition. Paul's response to their sufferings is indicative of his thought world. Far from lamenting, he declares them to be right on target: "For you yourselves know that we have been appointed to this, for even when we were with you we said to you beforehand that we were to be afflicted, just as it has happened and as you know" (1 Thess. 3:3-4; cf. Phil. 1:29). As the old aeon and its structures pass away and the new creation emerges, believers should not be shaken by the experiences of opposition and affliction; rather, these experiences should serve as indicators that believers are on their appointed path. Whatever else may be said about suffering, this conviction must be kept in mind.

Just as opposition and affliction are signs that believers are on target, they are also indicators that Paul is living as he should. His lists of hardships testify to his ministry's authenticity (2 Cor. 11:21-29 and parallels) and his faithfulness to his calling. His personal suffering convinces him that power and true comfort belong to God (2 Cor. 1:3-11; 12:9). Accordingly, he and all other believers are in the ironic position of rejoicing in their suffering, for with suffering comes God's comfort, which increases with greater suffering (2 Cor. 1:5, 7; cf. 1 Cor. 10:13). Affliction becomes the occasion for rejoicing because (1) it functions as an indicator that the believer is properly aligned with the new creation whose birth pangs are present and real (Rom. 8:18-24); (2) it identifies those with the patience to endure and those with the proper allegiances (Rom. 12:12; 1 Thess. 3:3); (3) it strengthens hope by indicating that believers are not far from deliverance and vindication (Rom. 5:3); (4) it highlights the believers' powerlessness, enabling them more clearly to see that the real power resides with God (2 Cor. 12:9); and (5) as affliction increases, so does God's graceful comfort. Suffering, hardship, and affliction, therefore, are gauges of one's identification with faith and the life of the Spirit.

Paul's treatment of affliction is always descriptive, never prescriptive. Suffering is never the goal of life; nowhere does Paul advise his readers to seek out affliction. Rather, because their commonwealth is in heaven believers living their calls will find themselves at cross purposes with the structures and powers of this age.

To some in the first century, suffering was an indication of sin and God's judgment (cf. John 9:1). By contrast, in Paul's thought world, the suffering of believers is not a sign of sin or of the absence of God. On the contrary, for Paul the suffering of believers is a sure sign of being in Christ, of belonging to God, and of being identified with God's new creation (2 Cor. 1:3-7).

Assumptions about Being Human

Although Paul clearly individuates in his reckoning about humans, some general assumptions about people do shine through in his writings. First, all humans are slaves of some power or force external to themselves. Paul's social world, where slavery was an accepted institution, gave him the image and no doubt prompted some of his understanding. The standing of a slave's owner or patron could bring the slave considerable power and therefore freedoms far beyond those of many free persons.

Accordingly, in Paul's understanding, true freedom is gained not by escape from slavery, but by the proper slavery—direct and full dependence upon God, whose power is beyond compare (Rom. 6:22). God liberates believers by freeing them from a wrongful slavery to sin and putting in its place a proper slavery to God. Christologically, Paul pictures the change of lordship as a slave market purchase (1 Cor. 6:20; 7:23). Even Paul's grammatical constructions express this understanding of human nature as dependent: Paul pictures people as "under" some thing or some power. Life without some master, lord, or authority is really unthinkable in Paul's time. There is an improper being-under and a proper being-under: "not under law but under grace" (Rom. 6:14-15). Improper being-under includes "under sin" (Rom. 3:9; 7:14; Gal. 3:22), "under law" (Gal. 3:23; 4:21; 5:18), and "under the elemental spirits of the world" (Gal. 4:3). For Paul, one may properly be "under grace," that is, living within the grace of God (Rom. 6:14-15).

One may deduce from this Paul's fundamental view of human nature: people are incomplete in and of themselves and therefore look outside themselves for some thing or some power to link onto that will give them significance. Faith is, after all, for Paul the proper relationship with God whereby the individual is dependently trustful that God will do what God has promised.

As Paul surveys the world around him, he sees that people have tended to enslave themselves to an improper dependence, whether it be to sin, to the law, or to the elemental spirits. God's grace in Jesus Christ offers release from such improper slavery and the possibility of another Lord.

PART TWO

MORAL REASONING

3

The Community as
Primary Context

We have no evidence that Paul ever conceived of a solitary, isolated believer. In his letters, admittedly written to communities of the faithful, he thinks of believers as called together in Christ.

He does, however, reckon with individuals within those communities: Philemon, the slave Onesimus, and Euodia and Syntyche (Phil. 4:2). There are also unnamed yet clearly identified individuals who were known to the recipients of Paul's letters: the famous brother (2 Cor. 8:18), the man sleeping with his father's wife (1 Cor. 5:1-5), and the one who did the wrong to Paul (2 Cor. 7:12).

On occasion, Paul may single out subgroups within communities for attention. Even in Rome, Paul, writing to churches he did not establish, addresses sometimes the Jews (Rom. 2:17-24) and other times the gentiles (Rom. 11:13-32). Writing to Corinth, he notes a problem that is caused more directly by the wealthy (1 Cor. 6:1-8). He recognizes that some within the community of faith may be weak while others may be strong (Rom. 14:1-12).

Whatever notice Paul takes of individuals or subgroups within the community, however, his primary context for thinking about believers is the community. He labors assiduously to maintain and edify the communal fellowship. The community is, after all, the matrix within which individual lives of faith are nurtured and maintained.

The Basis for Community

Paul's fellowships of believers were not brought together on the basis of a common socioeconomic background or a shared political outlook. Neither were Pauline fellowships structured out of similar religious or cultural backgrounds. Paul's followers, no matter what city they inhabited, were brought together by their shared death with Christ. They are the ones "in Christ," the ones for whom Christ died. They are the "work of God" (Rom. 14:20). This basis for community is expressed clearly in Paul's counsel about how one's behavior bears on or affects another believer. Paul's base-line affirmation in Rom. 14:15 is that believers must not "destroy that one in behalf of whom Christ died." The same argument is made to the Corinthians: "For the weak person is destroyed by your knowledge, the brother on account of whom Christ died" (1 Cor. 8:11).

Believers were of different social standing when viewed in terms of the old aeon. While most of the Corinthian faithful were not well born or of high status in the world, there were exceptions, for example, Erastus, Corinth's town treasurer (Rom. 16:23; 1 Cor. 1:26). Slaves and free persons were equally welcome. Believers had different religious and ethnic backgrounds: Jews and former adherents of gentile cults were welcome. They could be strong or weak in faith (Rom. 14:1). But most importantly for Paul, they had to welcome one another *because God welcomed them* (14:1, 3; emphasis added). As Paul wrote, "Therefore, welcome one another, just as Christ has welcomed you, unto the glory of God" (15:7). "Quarrels about opinions" (14:1) are not the reasons believers come together.

The Letter to Philemon illuminates Paul's understanding of community. Onesimus, the formerly worthless, perhaps even thieving, slave is reintroduced to Philemon as a new "beloved brother" in Christ (Philemon 16). Onesimus must be reintroduced, because since Philemon last saw him Onesimus has become a believer under Paul's tutelage. Philemon, known for his great love, is called upon to receive Onesimus back into his household in love, as a brother. By dying with Christ, Onesimus has become a part of the body of Christ; other details of his past are irrelevant.

Being Called

The beginning of the new life in Christ comes with a call. That call intercepts each individual just as and where she or he is. Gentiles remain gentiles — they do not need to be circumcised. Jews remain Jews. Slaves remain slaves unless the opportunity for manumission presents itself. Unmarried people need not marry; married couples need not become or act as if single (1 Corinthians 7).

The worth of the individuals who together form the community of the faithful is established by God, who in Christ began a work in each of those individuals. They are important because God's grace is effective in them. Called believers are given to one another in Christ and therefore are responsible for each other. They are actively to seek the good for each other (1 Cor. 10:24; Phil. 2:20).

Being "in Christ"

Paul's most frequently and variously used metaphor is "in Christ." Whether stated in its fuller form, "in Christ Jesus," or in the formulation "in the Lord," the metaphor describes the locus of the new life, the space made possible by God's grace. In so doing it becomes a means of identifying the persons who live there as those who believe, those who are included in the churches (1 Thess. 4:16; Phil. 1:1; 4:21; Rom. 16:11). Being "in Christ" is depicted by Paul as being "dead to sin but alive to God" (Rom. 6:11; cf. 1 Cor. 15:22). Those who are "in Christ" are sanctified, that is, set apart for God "in Christ Jesus" (1 Cor. 1:2). They are therefore not only freed from sin but also liberated from its attendant condemnation (Rom. 8:1). Accordingly, they live in freedom (Gal. 2:4; cf. 5:1).

Paul's references to being "in Christ" affirm the unity of believers. Paul found this affirmation in the baptismal formula he inherited from church tradition: "There is neither Jew nor Greek, there is neither slave nor free, there is neither male nor female; for you are all one in Christ Jesus" (Gal. 3:28 RSV). Similarly, Paul's image of the faithful as a body lets him recognize the variety of "members" while still affirming their place in "one body in Christ" (Rom. 12:5; cf. 1 Cor. 12:12-13). Identity and unity are affirmed.

In Christ, believers have an equality that is grounded in the grace of God. All believers recognize that in their prefaith days they were subject to sin. Now they know themselves reconciled — that is, justified — by grace through faith. Believers are equally in Christ; they have equal standing in Christ before God. All believers understand that if they stand firm in their faith they shall be granted the full inheritance at the Parousia of Christ. So even though Paul is not blind to their differences, believers are in many respects seen as having a fundamental equality.

Where there are differences of need, for instance, Paul expects those who have more to share with those who have less. That is the way he understands his collection for the poor in Jerusalem.

> Not that others should have relief and you be burdened, but in fairness
> your abundance linked with their lack, and so that their abundance may
> meet your lack — thus there may be fairness. (2 Cor. 8:13-14)

Fairness, or equality (*isotēs*), suggests that those who have should
help those who are in need; time and changed circumstances may
cause the stream to flow in the other direction. Presupposed is a
mutuality and reciprocity that is responsive to need.

Scripture instructs Paul on this issue: no matter how much
manna the wandering Israelites gathered each day, there was
nothing left over and no one lacked what they needed (2 Cor. 8:15;
cf. Exod. 16:18). The implication for the Corinthians is that having
more than one needs is not appropriate and that meeting the needs
of those in want is a scriptural principle.

The Letter to the Romans shows the results of this appeal: Paul
has a collection "for the poor among the saints at Jerusalem" (Rom.
15:26 RSV) that has been pulled together from among some of his
predominantly gentile congregations. He remains convinced of the
same mutuality and reciprocity of believers that he mentioned to
the Corinthians:

> For Macedonia and Achaia . . . were pleased to do it, and indeed they are
> in debt to them, for if the Gentiles have come to share in their spiritual
> blessings, they ought also to be of service to them in material blessings.
> (Rom. 15:26-27 RSV)

There is reciprocity and mutual support at work among the
believers, even across considerable geographical distance.
Believers belong to one another in Christ. Believers are to care for
one another as members of the same body.

The Philippians, by sending assistance to Paul, show their own
practice of Pauline reciprocity and support. Paul welcomes the
assistance, admitting his need (Phil. 4:11). Paul is confident that, as
the Philippians have met his needs with their assistance, so "my
God will supply your every need according to his riches in glory in
Christ Jesus" (4:19).

"In Christ" also designates the point of contact where God
engaged the world. Because the gospel is God's power and is made
clear and real in Christ, to be "in Christ" is to partake of God's
power as it has encountered the world. Apostles and other believers
operate from that power base as they are "in Christ" (Philemon 8).

Grace is given "in Christ" (1 Cor. 1:4). "God was in Christ reconciling the world to God" (2 Cor. 5:19).

Paul's sense of being "in Christ" is best captured by understanding the phrase—and indeed much of his christology—as participatory. Believers participate in Christ; they have solidarity with Christ; they belong to Christ. For Paul, humans "belong" in one of two fundamental ways: they can belong to Adam and thereby be marked out for condemnation and death; or they can belong to Christ and be marked out for eternal life (Rom. 5:17; 6:23).

Solidarity with Christ is most often expressed by Paul in terms of being "in Christ," but on occasion he turns the expression around and thinks of Christ in the believers. "I live—no, no longer I, but Christ lives in me" (Gal. 2:20). The text then expresses much the same view as the "in Christ" claims: the power to live is granted through Jesus Christ "who loved me and gave himself for me" (2:20).

Paul chides the Corinthians because they live as if they do not know that Christ in them or in their midst is the bench mark by which their comportment is to be measured: "Test yourselves. Or do you not recognize that Jesus Christ is in you?" (2 Cor. 13:5). The same image functions powerfully in Paul's lament over the Galatians, who are being tempted to turn from his gospel: "My children, with whom again I suffer birth pangs until Christ be formed in you!" (Gal. 4:19).

Whether it is Christ who is in the believers or the believers who are in Christ, Paul affirms the believers' solidarity with Christ. Even the baptismal image of vestment, reflecting the early Christian practice of garbing the newly baptized, serves the same purpose in Paul's thought world: "But put on the Lord Jesus Christ, and make no provision for the flesh, to gratify its desires" (Rom. 13:14 RSV).

On two occasions Paul embraces pre-Pauline traditions and speaks of Christ's death in sacrificial terms: God put forward Christ as an "expiation by his blood" (Rom. 3:25 RSV); and "Christ died for our sins" (1 Cor. 15:3). Usually, though, in his correspondence, Christ's death is not one of substitution or "for sins" but is one "for" the believers: "Christ died for the impious" (Rom. 5:6); "Christ died for us" (Rom. 5:8). God gave Christ up "for us all" (Rom. 8:32). "This is my body which is for you" (1 Cor. 11:24 RSV). Christ "loved me and gave himself for me" (Gal. 2:20 RSV). In these expressions, all built with the same Greek preposition (*hyper*), "for" is used in the sense of "in behalf of" or "for the sake of," not "in place of" or "instead of." Because Paul sees Christ's death as \a benefit to the believers, Christ's being "for" the believers means he is the one who takes their side (Rom. 8:31; cf. 2 Cor. 5:20).

Believers, because of their common association "in Christ," are inextricably bound up with one another: Because believers, "though many, are one body in Christ, and individually members one of another" (Rom. 12:5 RSV), "if one member suffers, all the members suffer together; if a member is honored, all the members rejoice together" (1 Cor. 12:26; cf. 12:27). That this is a Pauline commonplace can be observed by its reiteration in the Letter to the Romans: "Rejoice with the ones who rejoice, weep with the ones who weep" (12:15). Whether other believers grow in faith or stumble, rejoice or weep, bears directly on all other believers' self-understandings as well as their comportment. In fact, one's moral choices must be made with consideration for the other members of the body.

> We the powerful ought to bear the weaknesses of the powerless and not
> to accommodate ourselves. Let each of us accommodate the neighbor
> unto the good, for the purpose of edification, for even Christ did not
> accommodate himself. (Rom. 15:1-3)

Individual and Community
at Odds

Throughout his letters, Paul regularly counsels care for the well-being of the community and shows great concern for the individual members of the body, even the weakest among them. But wherever there is a tension between an individual's or a subgroup's rights and the well-being of the community, he sides with the community and calls for the individual or subgroup to go along with the larger community.

Paul exemplifies this principle in his open reflection about his death in his Letter to the Philippians. He can see some advantage in death: he could be eternally with Christ, which appeals to him (Phil. 1:21, 23). But his own desires, as powerful as they may be, are not the only or even the primary consideration. When he asks himself how his death might affect his partners in the gospel he knows that "to remain in the flesh is more necessary on account of you" (1:24). Therefore, he directly and firmly announces his plan: "Persuaded of this, I know that I shall remain and stay on with you all, for your advancement and joy in the faith" (1:25). Paul always expects of his followers this respect for what is good for the community.

Paul's commitment to community may rest in and be explained by the ways the fellowship serves and assists the individual. Community is the locale of the life of faith until Christ's Parousia. Community is the nurturing context within which the individual is expected to live. There the individual is encouraged to grow, is edified by the love of others, is shored up in weakness, is consoled upon straying, and is called to account when behaving inappropriately. Along with the workings of the Holy Spirit (see chapter 10 below), the community of believers is the guiding and encouraging force to keep believers on course, to encourage a continuity in the life of faith. Just as surely as one does not snub the workings of the Spirit, one does not disregard the community in one's life of faith.

Sin, by its powerful grasp upon the individual, provided a continuity to the life of the sinner, withering the will and destroying the capacity for self-extrication. The Holy Spirit and the work of the encouraging and correcting community provides a continuity in the life of faith.

The life of faith, the life in Christ, must be lived in the context and care of others. By God's grace, believers are given to one another and for one another. Only in fellowship can they be called to task and nourished so that each may be sustained and may grow as much as possible.

For Paul, the life of faith cannot be imagined apart from community. Yet belonging to community in Christ does not shackle individuation. Rather, the distinctive marks of the individual find proper expression within the community of believers.

4

Each Believer as
Distinctively Marked

Paul never loses sight of the individual. As much as he emphasizes community as the context for the life of faith, he nevertheless pays considerable attention to the way individuals relate within and to that community. In many ways believers are alike — equally dependent upon God's grace and equally important and valuable in Christ. But believers are also distinctive; each has a particular identity that sets him or her apart. The recognition of this individuality raises the issue of how a given believer is integrated into the life of the community.

Call

Paul, ever insistent on God's grace preceding and being the ground of any human response of faith, pictures God as intercepting individuals and breaking through the barriers of their self-imposed slavery to sin. Paul expresses this variously as election (Rom. 8:28-30, 33; 11:7, 28), reconciliation (Rom. 5:10-11; cf. 2 Cor. 5:19), or justification (Rom. 5:9). For "grace to be grace" (Rom. 11:6) Paul consistently affirms that the initiative lies with God, who initiates the restoration of relationships with the individual by choosing or calling the person.

Though all believers are "called," each call is distinctive in important ways. First, each believer is called in medias res, in her or his own historical and social setting. In many respects it seems that Paul assumes that life — particularly as it relates to the structures that exist in society — can proceed largely as before the call. Persons who are called need not pick up stakes and withdraw from the world, as some Corinthians misunderstood (1 Cor. 5:9-11).

Rather, they are called to live the distinctive life of faith precisely in their web of social and historical circumstances (cf. Philemon 10 12).

Second, the call may have an assigned task. Paul himself is a classic example. His calling was to be an apostle, one who is set apart for a particular function (Rom. 1:1; 1 Cor. 1:1; 2 Cor. 1:1; Gal. 1:1), namely, taking the gospel to the gentiles (Rom. 11:13; Gal. 1:16). Though his extant letters never say so explicitly, we may infer that Paul believes that the judgment at Christ's Parousia will evaluate whether people have lived up to their calls. Therefore, he is often anxious concerning whether he is running in vain (Gal. 2:2; Phil. 2:16; 1 Cor. 15:10, 14; 1 Thess. 3:5) and whether his followers are standing firm in their faith. These people are the fruit by which his ministry, his response to his call, will be judged. They are Paul's crown, his award at the end of a race well run (Phil. 4:1; 1 Thess. 2:19).

All believers are called "not . . . for impurity, but in holiness" (1 Thess. 4:7). Although believers live in the world and its structures as they have before their call, they are now expected to live distinctively within those structures and within that old world.

Gifts

Each believer is given one or more *charismata* by the Holy Spirit. These gifts are distributed as the Spirit sees fit (1 Cor. 12:11). Each gift is intended to serve "the common good" (1 Cor. 12:7). Paul portrays himself as especially gifted in the *charismata* he lists in 1 Cor. 12:28 and Rom. 12:6: he is an apostle; he does what he describes as prophecy (1 Cor. 14:3); he characterizes himself as a teacher (1 Cor. 4:17); and he speaks in tongues more than any of the Corinthians (1 Cor. 14:18). He notes that he has also been given the *charisma* of celibacy (1 Cor. 7:7).

The believers, gifted in different ways, should employ their gifts for the well-being of the body (Rom. 12:6). The varied gifts amplify the different functions represented in the various members of the body (Rom. 12:4). By linking his description of spiritual gifts to his image of the church as a body, Paul is able to extend his observations about spiritual gifts. Paul employs the common contemporary device of having the parts of the body converse with one another (1 Cor. 12:14-26) in order to drive home his central point: as different as the gifts may be, such differences must not become a means of categorizing or ranking the believers. Each believer is equally important for the functioning of the body. In fact, Paul is so eager to make this point that his discussion strains credulity. His argument goes something like this: Be careful that you not misjudge some parts of the body as weaker, for they may in fact be indispensable. So also with less "honorable" parts — don't we clothe them and dress them up so that even they become more honorable (1 Cor. 12:22-24)? Paul's willingness to go this far in argument indicates the importance of his point. In his subsequent Letter to the Romans he returns to this theme and encapsulates much of it in one statement: "For as in one body we have many members, and all the members do not have the same function, so we, though many, are one body in Christ, and individually members one of another" (12:4-5 RSV). The unity that the believers experience comes from their being in Christ, not from their having the same function. Conversely, different ways of acting or different functions must be understood as appropriate within believers' unity.

Measure of Faith

Believers differ from one another in the strength of their faith. Paul talks about faith in two ways. The first is a relationship of trusting dependence, illustrated clearly by Abraham who, hearing the promise of God, simply believed and trusted God to do what God promised (Rom. 4:21; cf. Gen. 15:6). For Paul, faith is not what one believes so much as it is a *right relationship* with God. This sense of faith is not subject to differentiation among believers — it is equally available to all, and all who are in Christ stand equally within it. The alternative to this kind of faith is sin, the wrong relationship, characterized by enmity and alienation from God (Rom. 14:23). For Paul there is a clear choice: either faith or sin. Mark's picture of faith and unfaith coexisting — "I believe; help my unbelief!" (Mark 9:24 RSV) — is not shared by Paul (Romans 6).

The second way that Paul speaks about faith is as a gift granted in a certain measure to each believer by God. Thus, he writes about each person having a "measure of faith which God has measured out to each" (Rom. 12:3). This view of faith is apparent in Romans when Paul writes about how those who are "weak with respect to faith" (Rom. 14:1) and the strong (15:1) should relate to one another. Even Abraham fits this picture when Paul says of him that he "did not waver with respect to faith but grew strong with respect fo faith" (Rom. 4:20). The notion of faith as variable in strength may help us understand how Paul not only lists faith as one of the spiritual gifts (1 Cor. 12:9), but also urges people with the gift of prophecy to employ it "in proportion to faith" (Rom. 12:6), thereby implying that faith is variable in degree. It also sheds light on Paul's counsel to the Romans that whatever faith the believer has is between that individual and God and therefore is not subject to judgment even by another believer (14:22).

Both perspectives on faith are about the same faith, that is, about the right relationship with God. When considered over against sin, faith's counterpart in Paul's thought world, an individual is either in the right relationship to God or is not; one either has faith or one sins. That is the first sense in which Paul writes of faith. When faith is considered, however, within the two horizons marked by death with Christ and the Parousia of Christ, then Paul envisions faith in terms of strength or weakness and in terms of growth.

The understanding of faith as being weak or strong and as capable of growth fits Paul's thought world in which growth and maturity apply not only to the life of the individual but also to Paul's images of the church as buildings, fields, and bodies. So the Corinthians are dubbed "babies" whose growth is stunted (1 Cor. 3:1-2; cf. 2:6). They are like children with a father (4:14-15). Years later, Paul still prays for their "completion" (*katartisis*; 2 Cor. 13:9). Even the Philippians, as irenic as Paul's relationship with them has been, are the cause for Paul to remain in the world: "for your advancement [*prokopē*] and joy in faith" (1:25).

Paul indicates in other ways that he recognizes individual growth within the life of faith. Some believers are more advanced than others. Among the Corinthians, for example, Paul recognizes the distinction between a "spiritual person" and an "unspiritual person" (1 Cor. 2:14-15). The context shows that Paul views the "spiritual person" as mature and dependable in judgment. With the Galatians he acknowledges a similar differentiation: the spiritual people are the ones who take care of the weaker ones and restore them (Gal. 6:1). People are at different stages in their faith journey toward maturity; those further along should show special care and consideration toward those who are not as far along.

Even though Paul always identifies with those with strong faith, he acknowledges to the Philippians that his life, too, is marked by a pressing on toward maturity or perfection (3:12-16). Apostles, indeed, all believers, have lives marked by striving and growth. "Whatever mature people there are, let us think this way" (Phil. 3:15).

Paul's understanding of faith as a gift variable in strength fits his view of the faithful life as one of growth. Whatever faith one has is a gift measured out by God and exists between the individual and God. This relation to God must grow; faith should become stronger as time goes by. In the meantime, people with stronger faith must be considerate of those with weaker faith. Neither group should judge or despise the other; neither is better or worse than the other. Each believer is a steward before God of the faith that she or he has received. Like apostles, all believers can pray and work toward increasing the completeness of the faith of others.

Freedom and Rights

All believers share equally in freedom from sin (Rom. 6:18, 22). All believers have been set free for freedom (Gal. 5:1). As each individual has a measure of faith, so also each individual has a range of actions appropriate to his or her degree of faith. That is the individual's freedom. Some people think one day is better than another; others reckon all days as alike. Some eat only vegetables; others are omnivorous (Rom. 14:5-6, 2-3). Paul takes no side on these practices because the question of what one eats is not as important as the question of whether one has eaten with respect and thankfulness to God (Rom. 14:6; 1 Cor. 10:30).

The abuse of personal freedom by some Corinthians who chose to act without regard for the effects of their actions upon others prompted Paul to put himself forward as an example worthy of emulation. He asks: Can they imagine anyone freer than Paul (1 Cor. 9:1)? As an apostle, does he not have rights? Paul knows that he does and assumes that they know it too (1 Cor. 9:3-12). But Paul at his pattern-offering best steadfastly refuses to exercise his rights with the Corinthians and will put up with anything "rather than cause a hindrance to the gospel of Christ" (9:12) or cause others to stumble. Note that he does not "give up his rights." On the contrary, he repeatedly insists that they are his (9:4-7, 12, 15); but he chooses not to exercise them. Put in different terms, Paul does not give up his freedom. He has the freedom to take a particular action, but he chooses not to in concern for others.

So individual believers have rights and freedom that pertain to them before God. The responsibility to employ those rights so as not to cause anyone to stumble or not to put an obstacle in the way of the gospel belongs to every believer. Believers are free to put their faith into action in a loving fashion; they can express their freedom and exercise their rights in the gospel so long as they do not thereby cause harm to another for whom Christ died.

Now, perhaps, we are in a position to understand a puzzling feature of 1 Cor. 10:28-30. Paul imagines that a believer has been invited to an unbeliever's house for dinner. Someone declares that the main course has been offered in sacrifice to another deity. Paul, after swiftly counseling that the believer should abstain out of consideration for the other's conscience, is driven to interject: "What! Why is my freedom found fault with by the conscience of another? If I myself take part in thankfulness, why am I blasphemed concerning the thing regarding which I myself give thanks?" (1 Cor. 10:29-30). Paul's remark is made because two of his values have come into conflict in this situation. On the one hand, Paul firmly believes that when someone raises a question on the ground of conscience — even if that person is an unbeliever — then the believer should honor that expression of doubt and accommodate to it. On the other hand, Paul recognizes that the issue is never so much what one does but whether one does it with thankfulness, to the glory of God. Paul's interjection, affirming as it does the second perspective, is his laconic way of recognizing that to give way each time someone has a question of conscience may lead to a reductive situation in which the faithful cannot do anything without offending the conscience of someone else in the community. The issue then is how one can accommodate the conscience of others without sacrificing one's genuine freedom as a person of stronger faith. Paul seems to want to hold both together in a balance (cf. Rom. 14:16) that reduces the chance for conscience to be used as a tool for manipulation.

5

Faith Expressed as Love

As noted earlier, believers receive different measures of faith at the start of their lives in Christ. Surely those in Christ grow in faith at different rates, and presumably an individual may grow in faith faster at some times than at others. In any case, Paul expects growth and improvement (Phil. 1:25; 2 Cor. 13:9) to characterize the life of faith. Because faith and love are so intricately inter-related in Paul's thought, the need for self-evaluation is even more pressing.

Self-Evaluation

Faith expresses itself (Paul uses a term denoting work, *energoumenē*) in love (Gal. 5:6; cf. 1 Thess. 1:3). The right relationship to God gains expression, or works itself out, in love for others. Paul seldom mentions believers' loving God (1 Cor. 8:3); when one is in proper relation to God one will direct love toward other believers. Love is all that any believer owes another (Rom. 13:8).

Paul does not offer his followers a list of loving actions, properly identified and waiting for implementation. He does tell them what love will do: love will edify or build up another person (1 Cor. 8:1); love does not keep a scorecard (1 Cor. 13:4-7).

Because faith varies in strength from person to person and because love is faith at work, one can love in proportion to one's faith. To reckon precisely what actions might lovingly put one's faith to work, a person must accurately assess the measure of his or her faith. The strong link between that measure of faith and proper self-evaluation is clear in Romans, where, at the outset of the appeal, Paul urges "every one who is among you not to think too highly of oneself beyond what it is necessary to think" (12:3). Elsewhere Paul also cautions against overestimating one's progress in faith: "If someone thinks himself to be something while being nothing, he deceives himself" (Gal. 6:3). Accurate self-assessment is basic to the life of faith: "If someone thinks he knows something, he does not yet know just as it is necessary to know" (1 Cor. 8:2). The same concern is recast in a different image: "Therefore let the one supposing himself to stand watch out that he not fall" (1 Cor. 10:12). Standing and falling are eschatological alternatives related to God's ultimate judgment of individuals (Rom. 14:4; cf. Rom. 11:20; Gal. 5:1). A proper and accurate self-assessment that does not overestimate one's progress in the life of faith is critical to living properly before God.

Too high a self-estimation is also a concern for Paul in his Letter to the Philippians: "Not from selfishness, not from empty conceit, but with humility let each one regard one another as surpassing himself" (2:3). Did Paul so frequently emphasize the dangers of high self-esteem because he thought it more problematic than a low self-estimate? Paul's moral counsel often displays a tendency to play it safe, and his counsel of humility may be another example of this.

Low self-esteem caused problems at Corinth. Some of the Corinthians — perhaps a majority — became convinced of their lack of worth to the community and allowed the enthusiastic but powerful minority in the church to prevail. This prompted Paul to address the problem of low self-evaluation:

> If the foot should say, "Because I am not a hand, I do not belong to the body," that would not make it any less a part of the body. And if the ear should say, "Because I am not an eye, I do not belong to the body," that would not make it any less a part of the body. If the whole body were an eye, where would be the hearing? If the whole body were an ear, where would be the sense of smell? (1 Cor. 12:15-17 RSV)

In Paul's thought world all believers, regardless of their strength of faith or their self-estimation, are equally important to the well-being of the community. One's measure of faith should gain full expression within the community through love.

Comparison and Judgment

Because faith varies so much from person to person, comparison among believers is ruled out. Note how quickly Paul seizes on his

Corinthian opponents' tendency to compare themselves with other people: "But these who measure themselves with regard to one another and compare themselves with one another do not understand" (2 Cor. 10:12).

Judgment is viewed in the same fashion. "Who are you, judging the house servant of another? With respect to his own lord he stands or he falls" (Rom. 14:4). Believers share the same point of origin and self-definition: they are those for whom Christ died, those who have died with Christ. Believers share the same destiny: they must all stand before the judgment of Christ or God. Between their new birth and their maturity or adulthood, the faithful must navigate at their own pace and with their own grace-bestowed gifts, with love, respect, consolation, and encouragement for each other. Accurate self-assessment distinctly defines one's location in the journey from infancy to maturity of faith and provides a clear point of reckoning from which one can seek not only to grow, but also to engage lovingly and supportively with others as they traverse the same general course.

The Judgment Day

Accurate self-evaluation is the sine qua non for proper action and thereby is critical to any hope of escaping divine judgment. Self-evaluation anticipates the eschatological judgment of God and permits the individual believer to make a midcourse correction. God's wrath is already being unleashed in the world against wickedness (Rom. 1:18) and, Paul thinks, has begun to make its mark upon some Corinthians who have taken part in the Lord's supper without proper self-testing (1 Cor. 11:30). Self-testing can avert judgment and its associated punishment if it leads to self-correction. "But if we rendered a [correct, understood] decision about ourselves, then we should not be handed over for punishment" (11:31).

In this context one can understand the Pauline beatitude: "Blessed is the one who has no occasion to judge oneself in the things which one approves" (Rom. 14:22). True blessedness is a status conferred by God; such felicity occurs only when the decisions one makes provide no occasion for self-indictment and thereby, when accurately assessed, avoid God's judgment. Only God can confer blessing or commendation (2 Cor. 10:18), but the believer, with a renewed mind, can discern God's will and do it. The believer can thereby avoid God's judgment and can confidently hope to receive God's commendation.

Proper Load-Bearing

It is critical for individuals to know their place, that is, where they are with regard to their growth in faith. A child not only faces fewer options from day to day but bears a smaller load. No one can tell for certain where an individual is in growth except that individual. Across time individuals need to assess their own faith to see how strong or weak it is.

Paul's counsel to the Galatians to be gentle with those caught in trespass and to "bear one another's burdens" (Gal. 6:2) is followed immediately by a warning not to have an overly inflated view of oneself and by a reminder that "each one will bear one's own little cargo" (6:3, 5). Bearing another's burdens and showing gentleness to those caught in trespass require an accurate evaluation of one's own faith regarding how much strength one may devote to taking on someone else's burdens. Though Paul does not develop the idea, he implies that to overload oneself in an effort to be loving and helpful to someone else is not truly helpful to either person.

Believers must bear each other's burdens. How much burden each individual can bear is reckoned by evaluating one's own strength and growth of faith.

Determining God's Will

Although Paul is convinced that God has a plan and that its shape has become clear in Christ, believers still must determine what God's will is and how it bears on one's life in the world. Between their shared death with Christ and their anticipated resurrection like his at the Parousia, believers must determine and do God's will.

Scripture provides instruction regarding the divine will and how one ought to live (cf. Rom. 4:23-24; 15:4; 1 Cor. 9:10; 10:1-11). As surely as no one can act against the counsels of scripture and continue to live the life of faith, no one can cross into the territory delineated by the vice lists (Rom. 1:29-32 and parallels) and continue to live the life of faith. Paul treats the vice lists as established borders that are beyond dispute and in no need of justification. In fact, people who do such things "are worthy of death" (Rom. 1:32); they shall not inherit the kingdom of God (Gal. 5:21; 1 Cor. 6:9). Within the boundaries formed by the vice lists, however, deliberation concerning appropriate behavior is necessary.

The believers' renewed minds (Rom. 12:2; cf. Rom. 1:28) must be employed to seek out and apply God's will (Rom. 12:2). By choosing sin people formerly had darkened their senseless hearts (Rom. 1:21), which resulted in God's giving them up "to a mind that would not stand the test" (Rom. 1:28). God left those sinners, bereft of functional hearts and minds, "to do the unfitting things" (Rom. 1:28). With the new creation begun in Christ, however, believers' minds are freed to determine "the fitting things" to do (Phil. 1:10).

For Paul, God's will does not have an existence apart from real people in real circumstances. Even within the borders defined by the vices, believers do not have prescribed things that they must do in specific circumstances. Paul does not provide that kind of casuistry. Believers must determine God's will as they meet the everyday challenges of their lives. Paul says to the Romans: "Do not be conformed to this age, but be transformed by the renewal of mind so that you may determine what is the will of God, the good, the pleasing and the perfect" (12:2).

Discern and Test All Things

Important matters in Paul's thought world are often cast in maxims and gnomic sayings, that is, pithy, memorable statements. Because the Pauline maxims are so frequently incorporated in discussions of what believers are supposed to know and operate with reference to, we may assume they were a basic instructional device. Only as we discern the broad scope of Paul's thought world do we see the link between particular maxims and Paul's thought. For example, knowing as we do from Rom. 12:2 that the renewed mind is to test out, discern, and apply God's will, we can surmise the way in which the gnomic saying in 1 Thess. 5:21 fits into Paul's thought world: "Test out/discern all things; retain the good." The believer is a discerning tester not only of what might be determined to be God's will, but of *all things* — events, deeds, practices, everything. This discerning testing is done to sort all things so that the good can be distinguished and retained.

The maxim in 1 Thess. 5:21 makes no effort to answer the question, Good with respect to what? Nor does it need to. No doubt Paul has already conveyed this to the Thessalonians in his teaching, and we see enough of it in his letters to know how it works. The good is measured in two ways that are equally important and necessary. One inquires whether the action or matter is good in terms of its impact on oneself; is it appropriate to the individual? The other evaluates the impact of the contemplated action or matter on others. In both calculations, individuation plays an important role. In the first, the individual has to reckon the good with respect to his or her own measure of faith and particular spiritual gifts. In the second, a person must factor in others' strength of faith, where they are on the journey of faith from childhood to maturity and what the projected action or matter would add to or detract from the common good.

The Fundamental Task

How Paul chooses to talk about the believer's fundamental task varies according to his purposes and concerns at the time. When he is concerned with life offered as a living sacrifice to God, Paul thinks about obedience to God's will (Rom. 12:1-2). When his topic is how the believer, before God, relates to others, the discussion focuses on love, the form it takes and the ways it may be encouraged (1 Cor. 16:14). Doing God's will and showing love are alternative but roughly equivalent ways Paul describes the believer's fundamental task.

Philemon may serve as an example of how love must be reckoned by the individual. Philemon, known for his great love (Philemon 5, 7), is called to love in an unexpected situation. Paul says he could have commanded "what is proper" (*to anēkon;* v. 8), but Philemon's good is better achieved voluntarily than by compulsion (v. 14). Philemon is left to determine, with the encouragement of the church of which he is a part (v. 2), what form his love shall take. He is not tested to guess which choice is the hidden, *right* action, for conceivably, Philemon could show love through more than one option. Philemon has to decide which choice provides him with the fullest expression of his love in this circumstance.

Believers lose their conformity with the old aeon even though they still live within it. Their renewed minds enable them to figure out (*dokimazein,* which for Paul has a wide range of meanings, including discernment, examination, discovery, and approval) and do "God's will," as Jews might more readily speak of it, or do what is "the good," "the pleasing," and "the perfect," as gentiles are more likely to talk about it (Rom. 12:2). By the functioning of the mind renewed in Christ, the believer determines what action among the many possibilities might most fully and directly put his or her measure of faith into operation in the situation at hand.

Love's form cannot be determined in advance or prescribed by another person not only because faith is individuated as to its measure granted by God and its development in one's life but also because the situations of life are never identical. Before love comes to flower, that is, before God's will is done, an individual not only has to gauge his or her own faith, but has to weigh out a particular situation and assess what action might be appropriate to that situation.

6

Determining
Appropriate Behavior

How does Paul expect an individual to discern which options may or may not be appropriate? Let us begin by mapping out the territory within which a believer must choose and act.

Vices

The vice lists mark out the farthest boundaries of acceptable behavior. As Paul says, persons who do such things simply will not inherit the kingdom of God (1 Cor. 6:9; Gal. 5:21). Their deserved fate is death (Rom. 1:32). It is unthinkable for Paul that believers would do such deeds under any circumstances. *Porneia,* well translated by the encompassing notion of immorality, seems to be a focal term with which Paul associates vices and improper conduct (1 Thess. 4:3).

Sin's power darkens the mind, makes it fail to meet the test. Under sin's power a person does things that are improper (Rom. 1:28). In contrast, the renewed mind should do what is proper, or what Jewish moralists of Paul's time would call "God's will," what pagan moralists would call "the good, the pleasing, the perfect" (Rom. 12:2).

Conscience and Doubt

Within the common borders marked off by the vice lists are personal fences that delimit a given believer's sphere of possible actions. All of one's actions must be appropriate to one's measure of faith. Faith's proper sphere of action is marked off by the individual's conscience and doubts.

For the functioning of conscience, Paul himself serves as an illustration at one extreme. Paul had a "robust conscience," as one would expect of someone who regularly identified with the strong in faith. For example, he knows and is persuaded "in the Lord Jesus that nothing is unclean in itself, except to the one reckoning something to be unclean itself, to that person it is unclean" (Rom. 14:14). Although Paul's conscience does not raise the question of whether he can eat any particular thing, he can imagine that a person of weak conscience might see one of strong faith eating at the table of a cult deity and wrongly think that he too could join the festivities and not pay homage to the deity. Paul recognizes that such a mistaken imitation could lead to the destruction of the person of weaker faith and conscience. Conscience functions as a warning signal and gives the individual an opportunity to refrain from the contemplated action.

In Paul's moral reasoning, conscience does not play a primary role. It does not supplant the function of the renewed mind in sorting through moral choices. Rather, it seems to function as a possible warning or signal, questioning the propriety of a contemplated action. The believer should pay attention and refrain.

Though possibly not distinct from what he thinks of as conscience, Paul considers that doubts or waverings also mark off individual fences within the boundaries provided by the vice lists. Wherever the individual believer experiences doubt, the believer should not act. There is nothing wrong with doubting. It is only wrong for the believer to doubt and then to do the thing that prompted the doubt. Paul's reflections in Romans about what believers may eat show his thought: whoever doubts, yet eats, is condemned (14:23). Doubts function to show believers the limits of their measures of faith. As one's faith, like Abraham's, grows stronger (Rom. 4:20), doubts recede and the range of possible actions grows.

Certainty and Conviction

Paul stresses acting with confidence or certainty when doubt is not a factor. Sometimes he makes this point by doubling verbs: "I know and am convinced" (Rom. 14:14; cf. Phil. 1:25). At other times he expresses it in other ways: Abraham, the one who grew strong in his faith and about whom it is said that "no distrust made him waver" (Rom. 4:20 RSV), is described as "fully convinced" that God was able to do what God had promised (Rom. 4:21). Paul lays down the principle "Let each person be fully convinced in his own mind" (Rom. 14:5). Conviction marks out the territory that is clear from doubt. When one acts out of what one knows without doubt then one is in a clear territory of proper moral choice for Paul.

It follows that people with stronger faith have knowledge and clear convictions about a broader range of matters within which they may fittingly act; accordingly they will encounter doubt less immediately. Conversely, people of weaker faith will have a narrower scope of freedom within which they may act; their fences marked by doubt will be met much sooner.

Some of the Corinthians, swept up in zeal for Paul's gospel and thinking themselves to be of strong faith (1 Cor. 4:8-10), thought they had a clear understanding of Paul's moral counsel when they recited the maxim "All things are permissible" (1 Cor. 6:12; 10:23). Maxims, like bumper-stickers, compromise on the complexity of moral issues. They ignore the nuances of the argument and pro-vocatively stake out a claim. We can imagine Paul embracing the slogan that "all things are permissible" with the following qualifi-cations: (1) if the deed in question cannot be considered to be one of the vices; (2) if the action is appropriate to your measure of faith; (3) if you have no doubt or wavering about its appropriateness; and (4) if you are fully convinced that it is proper for you.

Paul countenances no risk. Some people of weaker faith, then, will be able to eat only vegetables. If, as they consider whether they may eat meat, any one of the four tests fails them, they must abstain from the meat and eat only vegetables. At issue in each decision is the standing of one "for whom Christ died" (1 Cor. 8:11), and each person will have to "give account of himself to God" (Rom. 14:12 RSV).

In Paul's thought world believers cannot simply be divided into those with strong faith and those with weak faith. Instead, believers are to be found along what amounts to a continuum from babies in the faith (1 Cor. 3:1-2) to those who are reaching maturity or adulthood in their faith (Phil. 3:15). In Paul's understanding, Abraham, by growing strong in his faith, progressed along this con-tinuum (Rom. 4:20). The Corinthians should have been further along it than they were (1 Cor. 3:1-2). The Galatians worry Paul because he fears that, having gotten off to a good start, they may be about to lose their impetus (5:7) if not the very ground that they had gained (3:3; 4:8).

When faith grows and the area of doubt shrinks, believers must adjust their actions accordingly. What might have been appropriate or inappropriate at an earlier time must be reassessed in the context of the growth in faith that has occurred since that time. In order to know just how strong one's relationship to God is and what actions are appropriate to one's current measure of faith, one must constantly be self-reflective. Self-testing and self-evaluation are fundamental to the life in Christ.

The Call to Love

The Pauline moral test (discussed on p. 59) is not the final determinant of moral action, even though each of the steps is vital. A contemplated action may clear every check and still not be appropriate because one further test must be passed: Does the contemplated deed work love toward others? So far, within the borders provided by the vice lists, the questions have borne upon the self: Is the action appropriate to *my* measure of faith? The freewheeling Corinthians understood this correctly and probably expressed it in their own version of the slogan, "All things are permissible *for me*" (1 Cor. 6:12; emphasis added). Paul's additions to the Corinthians' slogan indicate the larger vista of Pauline moral reflection. All things may be permissible, but "not all things are helpful" (1 Cor. 6:12; 10:23), "not all things build up" (10:23). Projected deeds have to be evaluated in two ways: how they bear on the one who might do them and how they bear on others in the community of faith. It is not enough to ask whether some action might be appropriate to oneself, one must also ask whether the deed would help build up others in the body of Christ.

"Love builds up" (1 Cor. 8:1), so the ultimate test of a projected action is whether it shows love to others, whether it edifies others. Even if one could do the deed, satisfying all the tests with regard to oneself, the deed must be reckoned inappropriate if it does not give expression to love for the others within the community.

I have portrayed Paul's moral reckoning as if it had two moments, one relating to the individual, the other to those in the community who might be affected by the contemplated action. These two moments are in fact intrinsically linked. The first moment centers on faith and the freedom one's faith allows or does not allow; the second centers on love and how one puts love into effect for the common good. We can see the link when we understand that for Paul faith, one's proper relationship to God, gains expression, or "works itself out" (Gal. 5:6), in love. So the first moment—what one's faith permits—leads directly to the second—how that faith expresses itself in love for others in Christ.

However well some of the Corinthians may have understood the first moment—and therefore been able to discern just how wide their moral choices were—they failed to understand that the second moment of love and careful consideration of others was not receiving adequate attention. Though the believer may be free to do the action in question, the suspicion that it might harm someone for whom Christ died ought to be sufficient to cause the believer to forgo the exercise of his or her personal freedom.

In 1 Corinthians Paul claims to exemplify in his own life the balance between the two moments. He knows that no one is more clearly due the rights of apostolic support than he (1 Cor. 9:4-12), yet he has never made use of that right with the Corinthians (9:12) nor does he expect to (9:15). From his own standpoint he has the full freedom and right to receive the support; with respect to the first moment of moral reflection everything checks out positively for Paul. Nevertheless, he eschews the exercise of that right because of consideration for the community. The test of whether the exercise of his right would be helpful to the Corinthians fails. For Paul, freedom without such discipline leads to chaos and harm.

Paul expects each believer to monitor a delicate balance regarding self and others; moral reflection is a constant feature of life. An action deemed inappropriate in one situation could be judged differently in another. Paul's letters show numerous examples of this: his refusal to accept support from the Corinthians even though on several occasions he received support from the Macedonians— once even while he was at Corinth and refusing Corinthian aid (Phil. 4:16; 2 Cor. 11:9); the much-discussed double judgment that Paul gives the Corinthians about whether they can eat meat that has been offered to idols (1 Cor. 8:4-6; 10:19-21; 10:25); Paul's hyperbolic claim that he would avoid eating meat entirely if it might help others avoid stumbling (1 Cor. 8:13); and his evangelistic practice of accommodating his life patterns to those of his hearers (1 Cor. 9:19-23).

Although Paul cannot imagine a situation in which any genuine believer could do one of the actions described in the vice lists, he does expect a wide range of actions by the faithful within the community. Nothing keeps variety from being a prominent characteristic of his followers; if anything, Paul seems to have gone to great extremes to preserve variety and permit the honoring of differences. What is to keep bedlam from breaking loose in Pauline communities? Love, that is, the acting in careful consideration for the well-being of others, functions as the governor that sets some limits to what might otherwise be runaway individualism. Love makes genuine community possible by recognizing and preserving the common bond that otherwise very different and differentiated people have in Christ. While Pauline communities lack uniformity in so many ways, they nevertheless have a fundamental unity at the base of their relationships and lives.

Indeed, "the love of Christ controls us" (2 Cor. 5:14 RSV). It sets limits to the free expression of individual rights. The Greek verb *synechō,* translated as "controls" in this sentence, also can mean "urges on" or "impels." The love of Christ, then, also impels believers toward other believers. The love of Christ engages believers with other believers so that their care and well-being becomes important.

The delicate balance between care for self and care for others, so important in Paul's moral reckoning, should shed light on his references to Lev. 19:18 — "You shall love your neighbor as yourself" — as epitomizing the law (Rom. 13:9-10; Gal. 5:14). The quotation (also used by Jesus; cf. Mark 12:31 and parallels) ties together two distinct strands in Paul's thought world. Although the love of neighbor is Paul's moral bedrock, this passage likely also strikes another note for Paul: in that verse the love of neighbor is parallel with, indeed it is reckoned from, one's love of self. Paul's moral reckoning has the same double focus: care for self and care for others are integrated through love.

Knowing oneself to be secure in the love of Christ gives a person the freedom to allow other believers to be true to their own measures of faith. Believers who love their neighbors as themselves will recognize that each neighbor has her or his own measure of faith within which to make decisions and act, and that accordingly their actions will be diverse and distinctive.

7

Testing, Judgment, and Discipline

Intertwined through different parts of Paul's letters are linguistically linked terms that function in related ways in Paul's moral discourse.

Discernment

Paul frequently uses the term discernment (*dokimazein*) to signify "sorting out," as one identifies and separates the good from the bad, the valuable from the worthless. The power of discernment is lodged in the mind renewed in Christ (Rom. 12:2).

Because Paul chooses not to advise believers to flee the world for a Qumran-like isolation, he must lead his followers on a walk through two intertwined aeons where someone's mistaken judgment could cause a person to stumble. So Paul expects the faithful to "test all things" and, having discerned which are good and which are bad, to "seize onto the good" (1 Thess. 5:21). This same kind of testing is recommended when Paul urges the believers to "discern what is the will of God, the good, and the pleasing and the perfect" (Rom. 12:2). The other terms here — "the good," "the pleasing," and "the perfect" — are broad terms that for Paul are synonyms for "the will of God." Paul, conscious that different readers might describe differently what it is that believers are supposed to discern or sort out by their testing of everything, casts his linguistic net as wide as possible. This is borne out when elsewhere he writes about sorting out "the things that really matter" (*ta diapheronta*; Rom. 2:18). It is especially clear in Philippians, where he discloses to his readers his prayer that they "abound more and more in knowledge and in all insight," that is, in the capacity to make informed moral judgments, "in order that you may sort out the things that really matter" (*eis to dokimazein hymas ta diapheronta;* Phil. 1:9-10).

Believers test not only their moral judgments but their own work: "Let each test out his own work" (Gal. 6:4). We have seen why this injunction must in Paul's thought world be in the singular and addressed to each believer. Others do not know one's own measure of faith, where one's own boundaries of doubts and conscience stand, or whether one has strong convictions. Another person would not even be sure whether one intended love toward the neighbor. The only thing that another believer could test for certain would be whether one's actions crossed over into those forbidden by the vice lists. So each person must test out his or her own work, as Paul urges the recalcitrant Corinthians to "test" themselves, to see if they are still "in the faith" (2 Cor. 13:5). Paul cannot test them, although he is distressed with them, and he may have strong suspicions that they would fail their self-test.

Paul (possibly drawing on Jer. 11:20) is convinced that God "tests our hearts" (1 Thess. 2:4). Whereas believers are not able to test others' works or hearts (the seat of willing), God can. In fact, self-testing is designed to provide the occasion for self-correction and a change of course so that the final, eschatological test of judgment day will not be a surprise. In 1 Cor. 3:13, a passage bristling with images of judgment day, Paul anticipates the end time when each one's work will be manifest and when "the fire will test what sort of work each one has done" (RSV).

Believers make their way through this world figuring out what among human options is appropriate to God, fitting for themselves, and loving of their neighbors. Throughout their lives, up until the judgment day, believers also test themselves, their work, their hearts, and their standing in the faith. If they assess themselves properly, then they will know at any given time exactly what strengths and what weaknesses they bring into any relationship with other believers and accordingly what load they can reasonably bear.

For Paul, the blessed ones are those who can find no fault with themselves regarding what they sort out and act upon (Rom. 14:22). The blessed person not only has the assurance of being in line with God's will in the present time, but also can put aside any anxiety about God's final judgment.

"Tried and True"

The ones who have passed the test are the "tried and true" (2 Cor. 13:5-7). In Paul's picture of things, some people emerge over time as the ones who have proved themselves. "Tried and true" is a good translation of the term *dokimos* because it suggests a testing and a proving true in and through the test. In his struggles with the Corinthians, Paul sees that some "have passed the test" while others have failed.

Paul's opponents want to seek the "proof of worth" in him (*dokimēn;* 2 Cor. 13:3), but he turns the tables on them, asking them to "test" themselves (13:5). As much as Paul labors to overcome divisiveness in the community at Corinth, he does admit at one point that factions or parties (*haireseis*) do not surprise him; they are "necessary so that *the tried and true* among you may be plainly seen" (1 Cor. 11:19, emphasis added). Of Timothy, for example, he says, "You know his established worth" (*dokimēn;* Phil. 2:22). This use of the term suggests a certain *gravitas* that a person establishes over a period of time and through heavy responsibilities or in a rugged trial. Apelles is apparently such a person (*ton dokimon en christō;* Rom. 16:10). But Paul is careful: however much people may sort out those whom they think are tried and true, all such human reckonings are provisional and conditional "for not the one who commends himself is tried and true, but the one whom the Lord commends" (2 Cor. 10:18).

Paul also uses the term *epainos* to suggest "approval" or "recognition." Discerning believers can tell when someone stands out (cf. Phil. 4:2-3). The unnamed brother in 2 Corinthians who is "recognized in the gospel throughout all the churches" (8:18) is an example. He is being sent along with the collection and another unnamed brother who has been tested and found tried and true (*edokimasamen;* 8:22). Even so, the only recognition or approval that finally counts is from God, not from people (Rom. 2:29; 1 Cor. 4:5).

Disqualification

Paul employs the term "disqualified" (*adokimos*) for those who are not tried and true. In an athletic metaphor, he hopes that he will not ultimately be "disqualified" (1 Cor. 9:27) because of a lack of self-control (9:25). That would rule him out of the race and would mean that he had no chance at the prize (1 Cor. 9:24; cf. Phil. 3:14). To be *adokimos* is to fail the test; it is to be outside the border of appropriate conduct (Rom. 1:28). Little wonder that a mind that fails the test because of its servitude to sin is mentioned by Paul (Rom. 1:28) immediately before one of his most detailed vice lists (Rom. 1:29-32).

To fail in one's self-assessment, to fail in the living of one's faith, is possible for those in Christ. Believers must be on guard against self-deception because they may be led to act in such a way as to be disqualified — and that could lead to their crossing the border of acceptable conduct. Those who cross that border should be treated as outsiders (1 Cor. 5:11).

Judgment and Discipline

For Paul, some kinds of judgment are improper while other kinds of judgment not only are proper, but are expected of believers. The former is more frequently addressed in Paul's letters, so I will begin with it.

Improper Judgment

People have no business judging or evaluating another's faith. Faith is a granted relationship between God and a person and its strength is measured out by God. "Who are you, judging the house servant of another? With respect to his own lord he stands or he falls. But he shall stand, for the Lord is able to cause him to stand" (Rom. 14:4). Furthermore, human judgment preempts God's judgment at the end time when "*each* of us must reckon accounts *concerning himself*" with God (Rom. 14:12, emphasis added; cf. 2 Cor. 5:10; Rom. 2:16).

God's judgment is individuated because each person is responsible for his or her disciplined stewardship of the trust that God has granted (cf. 1 Cor. 9:24-27). Each person will give account directly to God who alone knows the secrets and purposes of the heart. "Therefore, do not judge before the time, until the Lord comes who shall bring to light the hidden things of darkness and shall reveal the hearts' plans" (1 Cor. 4:5). Preemption of God's eschatological judgment is ruled out (Rom. 14:10) because others cannot know the deliberations and purposes of the heart as the individual reckons what actions might be appropriate to his or her own measure of faith, or as the individual assesses doubt, conscience, and conviction.

Scorn also is ruled out: "And why do you reject your brother with contempt?" (Rom. 14:10). Instead, believers should welcome others "just as Christ has welcomed you" (Rom. 15:7) and be sure not to place a stumbling block (*proskomma*) or obstacle (*skandalon*) in their way (Rom. 14:13). Believers should focus on matters that are truly within their control: they should work to love others and be careful not to cause them to stumble.

Proper Judgment

Although most of Paul's comments about judgment are associated with the Parousia of Christ, there is some attention in his letters to what he considers proper judgment. Although he does not state it in detail, Paul knows that the believers are to take part in the judgment of the world at the end of time (1 Cor. 6:2) and that they are also then somehow to judge angels — whatever that may mean (6:3). He thinks the Corinthians should understand this, and it is beyond his comprehension that they cannot sort out "ordinary matters" (*biōtika;* 6:3). Instead, he laments, they rush to judgment in the presence of unbelieving judges who are not specialists in righteousness and justice as believers should be (6:6). The standing of another before God is not subject to judgment; however, in the "ordinary matters" of contention between individuals, judgment ought to be brought to bear and there should be someone wise enough to judge such matters (6:5). Failing that, believers should simply let themselves be defrauded (6:7). This perhaps ironic counsel is another example of Paul's predisposition to play it safe in matters where the well-being of another and of the community may be at stake.

In Paul's thought world, judgment of outsiders is not the task of believers, and judgment of other believers is generally thought to be out of order except when actions violate the boundaries constituted by the vice lists.

Paul employs judgment in writing about the man who is "living with his father's wife" at Corinth (1 Cor. 5:1-5). Paul declares with apodictic force: "For I, though absent in body but present in spirit, have already passed judgment as present on the one who has perpetrated this thing — in the name of the Lord Jesus" (5:3-4). Paul has received a report of this person's actions and identifies them as immorality *(porneia)*. In fact, the *porneia* is so blatant as to be of a sort that is "not even among the gentiles" (5:1). There is no question that the man has flagrantly violated the border within which believers must assiduously stay. This violation no doubt accounts for Paul's recitation of a vice list a few verses later (1 Cor. 5:9-13) in which *porneia* plays a prominent role (cf. 2 Cor. 12:19-21; Gal. 5:19-21). Here one is dealing neither with the secrets of the man's heart nor with his reckonings of what is appropriate to his measure of faith.

At issue for Paul is the health, or the wholeness, of the community (1 Cor. 5:6-8). To compound Paul's distress, some of the Corinthians are "puffed up" with boasting (5:2, 6) when, given Paul's earlier special instructions (5:9-10), they should have mourned (5:2) and withdrawn from fellowship with the man. Such border violations run the risk of infecting the community. Believers' holiness is bestowed upon them as a trust, given into their care. Discipline of the border-violators is in order as a means of honoring believers' having been washed, sanctified, and justified (1 Cor. 6:11).

But even judging insiders such as this Corinthian man is in some sense provisional: it is designed to turn him over to the judgment of God. Paul has the conviction that "God judges the people outside" the church. Once again, scripture is Paul's guide: "Drive out the evil person from among you" (1 Cor. 5:13; Deut. 17:7). How does one do God's will in a situation like the one in Corinth? Because the borders of the community clearly have been violated, Paul makes the judgment in the Lord and expects the community to assemble in the same spirit and drive out the evil man from them, as scripture suggests. The man will be expelled from the community and will therefore be exposed directly to God's judgment. Such discipline leaves the man with no self-imposed delusions regarding good self-assessment and community sanction. Paul supposes that all this may ultimately result in the man's being "saved in the day of the Lord" (1 Cor. 5:5).

Believers are to judge and avoid those who disregard the community borders indicated by the vice lists. "I wrote to you not to associate with any one who bears the name of brother if he is guilty of immorality or greed, or is an idolater, reviler, drunkard, or robber—not even to eat with such a one" (1 Cor. 5:11 RSV). As strong as the first part of 1 Corinthians is regarding proper judgment and discipline, the remainder of the letter conforms to the Pauline pattern that judgment is out of order with regard to individuated moral practice, such as what one eats, and on reckoning the importance of any particular gifts for the well-being of the body.

Conscience and doubt provide a double buffer, fencing the believer ever away from actions that resemble the vices. For Paul, the man living with his father's wife is clearly beyond the pale. The other believers cannot be allowed to tolerate such a flagrant border violation.

Most community interaction thrives safely within those borders. When a violation occurs, Paul hopes for repentance. Whereas a writer such as Luke views repentance of sins as a condition for becoming a believer (cf. Luke 3:3; 5:32), to Paul repentance functions at the juncture of a believer's misbehavior, remorse, and desire for reinstatement within the community of believers. Paul's convictions are stated clearly when he tells the Corinthians he fears he "may have to mourn over many of those who sinned before and have not repented of the impurity, immorality [*porneia*], and licentiousness which they have practiced" (2 Cor. 12:21 RSV).

When community borders are violated, grief is produced. For Paul, two kinds of grief are possible. One is the "according-to-God grief." This grief, temporary in duration, leads to repentance (2 Cor. 7:9), restores one to the proper track, and produces no abiding remorse — indeed it becomes the occasion for rejoicing (2 Cor. 7:9). Thus, "according-to-God grief" leads ultimately to salvation (2 Cor. 7:10). The other grief Paul calls "of-the-world grief" (2 Cor. 7:10). It "brings about death," signifying the presence of sin because for Paul sin leads to death with formulaic dependability (Rom. 5:12; 6:16).

Although one's self-tests are important and judgment within the community must be held within proper bounds, all believers ultimately will face divine judgment. God's or Christ's end-time judgment is not a fearful prospect precisely because of the believer's capacity for self-assessment. The judgment is, however, an important feature of the consummation of God's purposes. It is therefore important that the believers know precisely what it is that will be sought for and examined in the last judgment.

8

The Last Judgment as Recompensive

Paul is convinced that at Christ's Parousia each believer, himself included, will have to appear before the judgment bench of Christ (2 Cor. 5:10) or God (Rom. 14:10). There each person will have to "reckon accounts" individually (Rom. 14:12). Recompense will be granted each person on the basis of "the things which he has done in the body, whether good or bad" (2 Cor. 5:10).

Judgment and Works

In Paul's thought world, surviving the end-time judgment depends on the works the believer has to offer. The individual will not be shielded by the community's overall performance, nor is some blanket protection granted by Christ that is sufficient to steer one successfully past responsibility. For Paul, not even faith is the key to eternal access to God's presence such that one's having it would merit inheritance of God's kingdom. What one does while in the body and how one lives out one's faith — those are the concerns Paul expects to dominate the judgment. Paul's understanding is shaped by his experience: one does work and receives wages. So it is in the life of faith. The end-time fire "will test what sort of work each one has done" (1 Cor. 3:13); if a person's work survives that fire the person will receive a "wage" or "reward" (*misthos;* 1 Cor. 3:14; cf. 3:8). Paul echoes scripture (Ps. 61:12 LXX; Prov. 24:12) when he tells the Romans that God "will repay to each person according to his works" (Rom. 2:6). Satan's ministers, masquerading as agents of righteousness, shall have an end appropriate "to their works" (2 Cor. 11:15). All those who do evil will receive "tribulation and distress," and "all who work the good" will receive "glory and honor and peace" (Rom. 2:9-10).

Paul also describes the reward as a prize such as an athlete would receive at the end of a well-run race. "Run in such a fashion that you may receive it" (1 Cor. 9:24). That is how Paul views his own life and work. He practices self-control (1 Cor. 9:25); he runs as someone who has a fixed goal and a clear picture of what can earn disqualification (1 Cor. 9:26-27). He strains toward what lies ahead and pursues "the prize of the upward call of God in Christ Jesus" (Phil. 3:14).

Paul's understanding of his call and the call of each individual believer accords with what we have already seen. How one lives one's call will be the focus of the judgment. In this regard, Paul's behavior is a good reflection of his thought world. At the Jerusalem conference Paul was concerned whether all his gentile converts would be accepted on equal standing with Jewish believers. His mission was not to create a separate group of churches composed of gentiles but to bring gentiles into the one people of God. If Paul's gentile converts were not accepted, then Paul's work would have been a "running in vain" (Gal. 2:2). Likewise, Paul's converts had to stand firm so that "in the day of Christ I may be proud that I did not run in vain or labor in vain" (Phil. 2:16 RSV; cf. 1 Thess. 3:5). In the climax of Paul's great exposition on the resurrection toward which believers strive, Paul concludes his appeal: "Therefore, my beloved brothers, be steadfast, immovable, always abounding in the work of the Lord, seeing that your labor is not vain in the Lord" (1 Cor. 15:58).

For Paul, faith leads to works—works never lead to faith. Abraham is Paul's model of the faithful person: Abraham simply trusted God's promise and so was justified. He was not justified by his works (Rom. 4:2). Paul quotes scripture: "God reckons righteousness apart from works" (Ps. 32:1-2; Rom. 4:6-8). One of his laments over his fellow Jews is that their pursuit of righteousness has not been through faith—the only access—"but as if it were from works" (Rom. 9:32).

Paul fears that the lamented mistake his fellow Jews have made is being reenacted by his Galatian (gentile) converts. He knows—and thinks the Galatians know too—that they have received the Holy Spirit. At issue is how they think they came to be granted the Spirit: "Was it from works of the law that you received the Spirit or from the hearing of faith?" (Gal. 3:2). Works, when cast in the phrase "works of the law," are always viewed pejoratively by Paul. Works, that is, performance, cannot bring a person into right relation with God.

Then how can it be that one's fate at the last judgment depends on one's works? Faith, once it is established by God's grace, expresses itself through works. Faith "works" (*energein*) through love (Gal. 5:6). The judgment will not assess one's faith because faith is meted out by God as a gift; if God were to judge faith, God would be judging God's own gift. Judgment, therefore, is based on the works that the individual has done, how those works fit and give expression to one's own measure of faith, and how those works bear on others. God alone knows the hearts' secrets and will disclose them on that Day (Rom. 2:16; 1 Cor. 4:5).

The anticipated final judgment and one's ongoing self-assessment are reciprocally related. Testing oneself along the way helps a believer accommodate the norms that will be employed at the last judgment. Believers know that God is on their side. They self-test and apply, in advance of that Day, the standards that they understand will be employed by God, whose judgment may nevertheless surprise them (1 Cor. 4:4).

All works that the believer does are finally and profoundly understood by Paul as enabled and powered by grace. One's works gain their significance as they become part of the working out of one's own salvation (Phil. 2:12); they matter only if they provide the basis for "commendation [*epainos*] from God" (1 Cor. 4:5) at the Parousia. Paul can urge believers to "work out" their own salvation precisely because God is already working in them (Phil. 2:13). This is the Pauline circle: believers work because God is already working; because God is already working, believers also work. So even the works upon which one will be judged in that Day are done on the power of God's grace.

Therefore, to boast of one's works is ultimately to boast of God's work. And to boast of one's works is to focus the moral life of faith onto the matters that are indeed within one's control, namely, what one does in the body. Thus, Paul can write: "But let each one test his own work, and then the boast he has is unto himself alone and not unto the other person" (Gal. 6:4). Paul, when he does boast, brags of his own labors and hardships (2 Cor. 11:21-28; cf. 6:4-6; 12:6). He does not want his readers to take pride in what they might cause someone else to do. For Paul, one would do better to pay attention to her or his own works, to see that one's faith gains expression in love. If one's works test out as acceptable, then one is blessed (Rom. 14:22) and has something truly boast-worthy.

Each believer has a "good" that belongs to that individual. It is intricately tied to what the person does. Philemon's good is best arrived at by his self-determination and deliberation: "but I wanted to do nothing without your approval in order that your good might not be by compulsion but by self-determination" (Philemon 14). Paul could command a particular action as appropriate (Philemon 8), but his love recognizes that Philemon must determine what is appropriate not only to Onesimus but also to himself (v. 9). Whatever work Philemon determines to do toward Onesimus will be part of his good. In Romans we saw that the believer, empowered with a renewed mind, was exhorted to determine and do God's will, which also was called "the good" (Rom. 12:2). In the Letter to Philemon there is no mention of "doing God's will," but the synonymous expression — Philemon has to do "the good" that is appropriate to him and to Onesimus — carries the same weight.

Perhaps this also helps explain why Paul, in the midst of arguing that one should always leave room for the distinctiveness of faith and its actions among persons of varying strengths of faith, intrudes with "However, do not let them deride your good" (Rom. 14:16). To attack a person's good is equivalent to undertaking the wrong kind of judgment because one's good is directly structured from one's measure of faith and what action might be appropriate to that faith. Neither should believers countenance any attack on their own good. Paul believes that accommodation to the needs of others ought to be a fundamental guideline of conduct within the community of believers, but that such accommodation ought in no way to come at the expense of compromising one's own good.

"Things Pertaining to the Other"

We can now add one more consideration that is operative for Paul: when there is a conflict of interest between individuals within the community, each person should be guided by a willingness to seek the things that pertain to the other. "Let no one seek the things pertaining to himself but the things pertaining to the other" (1 Cor. 10:24). A similar counsel appears in Philippians: "Let every one of you look out not for the things pertaining to themselves, but every one of you also for the things of the others" (2:4). The inclusion of "also" (*kai*) in the second part of the statement indicates that the injunction in the first part is not absolute. Believers retain some basic consideration of matters pertaining to themselves, but Paul wants each believer to be especially attentive to the matters that pertain to others in Christ. If everyone is eagerly seeking to secure what is in the best interest of the others within the body, then all will benefit. If all believers defer to one another (Phil. 2:3) then no one will be trampled on or left out. If they are considerate of others, then maximum encouragement and edification will be accomplished.

Although Paul takes for granted that care for oneself is appropriate to the life of faith, when he confronts a community situation he regularly calls for people with stronger faith to be considerate, even deferential, toward those with weaker faith.

> We the strong ought to bear the weaknesses of those who are not powerful, and not to accommodate ourselves. Let each accommodate to the neighbor unto the good, for edification, because Christ also did not accommodate himself. (Rom. 15:1-3)

Here we see two important Pauline concerns allied with one another: achieving the good and edification. When one aims for the good, one is being built up. Encouraging the neighbor to achieve the good, or in other words, edifying the neighbor, must come before self-accommodation.

We can see a pattern in Paul's counsels. Whenever Paul considers what is best for an individual, he concerns himself with that person's good, growth, and edification. Whenever Paul considers the individual in relation to others in Christ, he regularly counsels each person to pay special attention to the needs of others. Whenever one has an opportunity to accommodate the neighbor with respect to his or her own good one ought to pursue it. At no time does Paul counsel the sacrifice of one's own good in the encouragement of another's good, despite the Revised Standard Version's unfortunate translation of 1 Cor. 10:24. Each believer is to pursue her or his own good; each believer is to encourage other believers to pursue their own goods; and every believer is to pay special attention to the interests of others.

Paul's moral counsels are consistently conservative and low risk. Paul does not suggest that individuals test to see how far they might be able to go; rather, he thinks of borders within which believers ought to stay, and he constructs a fence wherever there is the least hint of doubt or twinge of conscience. Permeating his moral advice is the apparent conviction that it is better to play it safe.

His counsels to the Corinthians about marriage and human sexuality exemplify his inclination to play it safe. One of his main goals in that section of the letter is to maximize devotion in the last times (1 Cor. 7:26, 29, 31, 35). Within that goal he distinguishes doing better and doing fine. The "better way" (*kreisson*; 7:38) is refraining from marriage altogether—that way no interests are divided (7:32-34) and a person's will and heart are clear to function (7:37). Paul recognizes, however, that not everyone has that much self-control; sexual urges may be strong and therefore must be reckoned with. In such cases, Paul acknowledges that marriage is appropriate. To marry is to "do fine" if the better way is not open because of sexual desire (7:36). Even this "doing fine" is the best that a given person can do; therefore, the principle of playing it safe is still in evidence.

Another illustration of Paul's playing it safe is his advice to the Roman believers about how they should relate to governing authorities. Even though Paul may be indebted in part to a widespread Christian tradition of honoring governing authorities (cf. 1 Pet. 2:13-14, 17; Titus 3:1), he nevertheless delivers his advice in typically conservative style. His argument goes something like this: If you want to avoid trouble with governing authorities, then do the good and you will receive their commendation; you need to fear them only if you do the bad (Rom. 13:3-4). To live in such a fashion has two important consequences: believers can avoid offending their consciences and escape God's wrath (13:5). Although this moral counsel shows Paul's consistently conservative approach, it may also have been very practical advice for Roman Christians to keep a low political profile in a time when conflagration was soon to erupt, as it did in 64 C.E.

Walking in Faith

One of Paul's favorite images for living the life of faith is "walking." One who walks chooses certain paths and decides not to take others. One who walks moves from one place to another. Believers "walk in newness of life" (Rom. 6:4); they walk "worthy of God" (1 Thess. 2:12) and in such a fashion as to "please God" (1 Thess.

4:1). In fact, they should walk in such a way as to set a good pattern for others (1 Thess. 4:12; cf. Rom. 13:13).

As a Jew Paul thinks of life properly lived as a sacrifice offered to God. As persons claimed by God and thereby sharing in God's holiness, believers are addressed as "saints" (cf. Rom. 1:7 and parallels) and the lives they offer up to God are to be "holy" sacrifices pleasing to God (Rom. 12:1). Temple imagery expresses the same conviction: "For the temple of God is holy, which you yourselves are" (1 Cor. 3:17). "Flee immorality [*porneia*]. . . . Do you not know that your body is a temple of the Holy Spirit which is among you, which you have from God?" (1 Cor. 6:18-19). Paul views holiness as a standing, as a trust placed in the care of the believers. How they live determines whether their lives are offered up as a living and holy sacrifice; in their actions believers either honor the holy temple that God has granted them in their bodies or they violate it. If believers are to honor the temple which is their body and keep it holy as a gift from God, then they must flee *porneia*, Paul's all-inclusive vice. Holiness can be preserved as a trust only when it is kept clear from the contamination marked off by the vices.

9

The Focus as Doing
What Matters

Like a good Stoic, Paul, the apostle to the gentiles, used categories that his readers would readily understand. By Paul's time Stoics had a long history of trying to distinguish matters of great importance from ones that were of no consequence. Stoics urged individuals to pay special attention to important matters and to disregard or view with equanimity inconsequential matters. The only thing important for the Stoics was what was under the (wise) individual's inner, rational self-control. For Paul, as we shall see, what mattered was construed differently.

Distinguishing Things Indifferent

It may well be that Paul's ears, attuned as they were to Stoicism, heard in a special and powerful way the early baptismal formula that he recites most fully to the Galatians: "There is neither Jew nor Greek, there is neither slave nor free, there is neither male nor female; for you are all one in Christ Jesus" (Gal. 3:28). To be one in Christ transcends and neutralizes the powerful ethnic, social, and sexual distinctions. These formidable worldly differences are rendered as *adiaphora,* that is, transformed into indifferent matters.

Neither Jew Nor Gentile

All believers are one in Christ. Paul's participation in the Jerusalem conference (Gal. 2:1-10) and his efforts there reflect his deep conviction that the one gospel could not produce two distinct branches of the church, one Jewish and the other gentile. Similarly, the fatherhood of Abraham as it is expressed in Romans 4 stresses that Jews and gentiles who believe God are equally children of the promise (Rom. 4:11-12; cf. Gal. 4:22-31). Paul even expresses this conviction by idealizing circumcision along the lines of Jeremiah 31 (Rom. 2:25-27). He redefines what it means to be a Jew so that it depends not on lineage but on a circumcision of the heart that is possible also for gentiles (Rom. 2:28-29).

Clearly, in Paul's thought world circumcision and uncircumcision do not matter in Christ. Three times he explicitly casts this conviction as an *adiaphoron:*

"For in Christ Jesus neither circumcision means something nor uncircumcision, but faith expressing itself through love" (Gal. 5:6);

"For neither circumcision is something nor uncircumcision, but new creation" (Gal. 6:15);

"Circumcision is nothing, and uncircumcision is nothing, but keeping God's commandments" (1 Cor. 7:19).

Here circumcision stands for being a Jew, and its absence signifies a gentile.

What does it reveal about Paul's thought world that these three *adiaphora* maxims end in such distinctive ways? Because the three opening clauses so much resemble one another, a reasonable exegesis would be that the three last clauses — "faith expressing itself through love" (Gal. 5:6); "new creation" (Gal. 6:15); and "keeping God's commandments" (1 Cor. 7:19) — are largely interchangeable and mutually interpretive in Paul's thought world. One who is in Christ is a new creation (cf. 2 Cor. 5:17); one who is in Christ is in right relationship to God, namely faith, which gains expression through love; one who is in Christ discerns and does God's will, that is, obeys God and keeps the commandments of God. It does not matter to Paul whether one is a Jew or a gentile; what matters is whether a person is a part of God's new creation in Christ and lives accordingly.

Neither Slave Nor Free

Paul's social conservatism, powered by his imminent eschatology, caused him to assume that slavery would continue as a social institution until the impending end of history. In fact, Paul uses the image of slavery in order to express his gospel. He likes, for example, to picture himself as a "slave of Christ" (Rom. 1:1; Phil. 1:1; 1 Cor. 7:22) and Christ as the "master" or "Lord" who secured Paul and the other slaves by a transaction (1 Cor. 6:20; 7:23).

Those whose worldly social status was as slaves when faith came to them continue to be slaves when viewed from the standpoint of the old aeon; from the perspective of the new aeon, however, they are brothers and sisters in Christ (cf. Philemon 15-16). Paul expects all persons to stay in the stations of life where they were called (1 Cor. 7:20). "Were you a slave when called? Never mind" (1 Cor. 7:21 RSV). Although a slave could take advantage of an opportunity to be set free (1 Cor. 7:21), he or she need not worry about social standing: "For the slave who was called in the Lord is the Lord's freed-person; similarly, the free person when called is a slave of Christ" (1 Cor. 7:22). Being in Christ transfixes the categories of the world so that former social reckoning is erroneous — all those in Christ have been bought like slaves traded in the marketplace (1 Cor. 7:23).

Neither Male Nor Female

For Paul, sexual identity is a matter of indifference. Euodia and Syntyche are accorded the highest possible status when Paul identifies them with the rest of his "fellow workers" whose names are to be found in the book of life (Phil. 4:3). Phoebe, the deacon, is commended to the churches in Rome (Rom. 16:1-2). Chloe, whose agents help keep Paul informed of happenings in the church at Corinth, is a person whose status does not have to be argued to the Corinthians (1 Cor. 1:11).

Although Paul has problems with the comportment of some of the women at Corinth, he recognizes that they are praying and prophesying in the worship services and does nothing to stop those practices (1 Cor. 11:2-16). Many scholars think that 1 Cor. 14:33b-36 is a later redactional insertion designed to bring the Pauline text into line with the second-century practice of keeping women silent in the churches.

Paul's answers in 1 Corinthians 7 to questions about human sexuality and marriage show his deep commitment to reciprocity in relations between the sexes in Christ. His counsels are repeated, once to the men and once to the women, showing Paul's conviction that in Christ there is neither male nor female. As surely as "the wife does not have authority over her own body" so also "the husband does not have authority over his own body" (1 Cor 7:4). Advice to a believing husband married to an unbelieving wife is paralleled by the same counsel to a believing wife married to an

unbelieving husband (1 Cor. 7:12-13; cf. 7:14). The same reciprocal doubling is found in 7:16 and 7:32-34 (cf. 7:28).

Neither Life Nor Death

Life and death also are transcended by participation in Christ. It
is not just Paul's experience of being "near death many times"
(2 Cor. 11:23) that causes him to view death as an inconsequential
matter; a strong theological conviction is also involved. The key is
revealed in Romans: "we are the Lord's" (14:8). Believers belong to
Christ. Having shared a death like Christ's, they have already died,
and they are linked with the greatest confidence to Christ's resurrection. For believers, to die will simply mean to be with Christ
(Phil. 1:23).

Paul's imprisonment at the time of his writing to the Philippians
occasions some reflection about life and death. He ponders
whether he should go on living or die. In either case, he hopes that
"as always so now Christ will be glorified in my body, *whether
through life or through death*" (Phil. 1:20, emphasis added). Neither
death nor life has special value in itself; both pale in importance
before the question of whether Christ is honored in Paul's body.
Because of his relativistic view of life and death, Paul acts in the
following ways: (1) he is faithful to his call, so he preaches the
gospel to the praetorian guard and to "all the rest" (1:13); (2) he
reassures the Philippians that they should not be concerned about
his life or death, because either prospect has certain advantages
(1:21-22); and (3) he weighs his personal options of life and death
according to their bearing on others for whom Christ died and finds
that, though he would like to depart and "be with Christ" (Phil.
1:23; cf. 2 Cor. 5:8-9), it is "more necessary to remain in the flesh
on account of you" (Phil. 1:24; cf. 1 Thess. 5:10).

It is from his conviction that life and death are indifferent
matters for believers that Paul deduces his argument for the rela-
tive unimportance of days and of what a believer can and cannot
eat. Some believers hold certain days special; others consider all
days alike. To Paul this is an indifferent matter so long as reckoning
is done in honor of the Lord and thanks are given to God. The same
is true of eating or abstaining from certain foods (Rom. 14:6). To
seal his point, Paul turns to life and death.

> No one of us lives to himself, and no one dies to himself. For if we live,
> we live to the Lord; if we die, we die to the Lord. Therefore whether we

live or whether we die, we are the Lord's. For this purpose, Christ died and he lives, in order that he might be Lord both of the dead and of the living (Rom. 14·7-9)

Life and death, in and of themselves, have become indifferent matters—either may be fruitful for believers.

Other Indifferent Matters

Paul knows the vagaries of life. He gets along whether he has much or little.

> For I have learned, in whatever circumstance, to be content. I know how to be abased; I know how to be abundant. In everything and in all respects, I have been initiated into eating my fill and being hungry, to abounding and being in need. (Phil. 4:11-12)

Whether he is hungry or satiated, whether he has much or little—these are indifferent matters to Paul. When he needs support he either works with his hands or receives some help from a church from which he will accept assistance. He is granted strength to abide the full range of life's experiences: "I can bear all things in the one who empowers me" (Phil. 4:13).

Paul may have understood his imprisonments and illnesses in the same way. The imprisonment during which he wrote the Philippians is not of any special consequence for Paul except that it gives him occasion for preaching to a very different type of audience (Phil. 1:12-13). Similarly, his "chains" have let him become Onesimus's father in the faith (Philemon 10), but otherwise seem no burden. Paul notes that his illness in Galatia was a trial to *them*, not to himself (Gal. 4:14). To him it was a chance to preach the gospel to people that he apparently had not expected to reach.

What seems to have mattered most to Paul was that he respond to his call to preach the gospel to the gentiles. As long as he was responsive to that call, the other circumstances were "indifferent matters" that he could abide one way or the other. Whether he was in jail or free, whether he was ill or well, he could still preach.

God's being "for us" (Rom. 8:31), as Paul likes to put it, gives perspective to our walk through life between the aeons. If God is "for us" then who is "against us"? Who presses charges and condemns (8:33-34)? Whatever may happen, whatever others may do, nothing can separate the believers from the love of Christ or from God's love (8:35, 39). Paul stands persuaded that, with God's love securely in place, death, life, angels, rulers, present things, future

things, powers, heights, depths, and all other things of creation
(8:38-39) are robbed of their claims to power and reduced to
indifferent matters.

Through the *adiaphora*, the things that do not have ultimate
significance for moral life, Paul narrows his focus concerning what
is truly important. This clarity is fundamental to keeping one's
perspective within the two inimical aeons.

Although life and death are indifferent matters to Paul, he does
not discount the significance of what one does in life. Rather, Paul
chooses to become more involved in life and with people. Precisely
because life and death are neutralized in significance, Paul is free
to choose service to the Philippians as a way of life. Though this age
is of no consequence to Paul, it is the time in which he runs his race
and honors his call. Although the present is not Paul's destination,
it becomes the time when he glorifies God. Though the future has
no power over him, he aims for it with a certain zeal.

Adiaphora free the believer for genuine involvement in life with
others and guard against mistaken placement of values. Because
life and death are not the final arbiters, one can either face death
with equanimity or one can become very involved in life. With the
Philippians in view, Paul chooses to become involved in life,
although death has its attractions for him.

Discerning Things that Count

Paul expects the believer to discern what the important matters
are. His prayer for the Philippians distills much of his overall view
of things:

> And this I pray: that your love may abound still more and more in recogni-
> tion and in all insight, so that you may discern the things that really
> matter, so that you may be pure and giving no offense until the day of
> Christ. (Phil. 1:9-10)

Paul is confident that the Philippians profoundly share his thought
world. They have been partners in the gospel with him for years.
They and he understand one another. They do what they have
"learned and received and heard and seen" in Paul (Phil. 4:9). Paul's
prayer for them gathers up, in what is tantamount to technical terms
of moral discourse, much of what he thinks believers should do. To
start from the end, as Paul's moral reckoning does, all of one's moral
choices are made with the full knowledge that one will ultimately

be judged on Christ's day. On that day, the issue will be whether one is "pure" — the term *eilikrinēs* suggests sincerity or purity of motive — and "giving no offense," that is, taking one's moral steps in such a way that one has caused no offense to others (cf. 1 Cor. 10:32) and is therefore "blameless." Paul prays that their love may overflow — which presupposes that their faith is well established and operative — in knowledge or recognition (*epignōsis*), especially regarding moral issues, and in every experience (*aisthēsis*) so that they can discern (*dokimazein*) and do the things that really matter. That is the essence of the moral life for Paul. Love fills up one's life and informs all moral knowing and doing in such a way that one sorts out and does the things that really matter. Believers do what matters in such a way and with such consistency that their motives are not mixed and their performance does not cause offense or stumbling to others. Living thus, believers confidently arrive at the day of Christ with no fear of judgment.

With this background, we can read with insight Paul's ironic rebuke of his fellow Jew in Rome who has so much right in his view of things:

> But if you call yourself a Jew and find comfort in the law and boast in God and know [God's] will and figure out the things that really matter, being instructed by the law. . . . (Rom. 2:17-18)

The rhetorical form of this passage is as follows: How can you understand so many basic matters and be so eager to share them with others, and yet not benefit from your own insight and instruction? Paul thinks that a Jew ought to know God's will and, with guidelines from scripture, be able to discern and do the things that really matter (*dokimazeis ta diapheronta*). An important part of figuring out which things matter (*diapheronta*) is distinguishing the things that do not matter (*adiaphora*). Paul's letters show that he does this and expects his readers to do so as well.

PART THREE

HOW AND WHY BELIEVERS KNOW AND DO

10

Reasoning from What Is Known

How does Paul expect his followers to be able to discern the way they should live the new life of faith? To what resources does he expect them to turn? Paul assumes that his readers have considerable riches, and he refers to them across the corpus.

Renewal through the Spirit

Paul affirms that God's Spirit has been granted to every believer. Though believers may not "know how to pray just as it is necessary," the Spirit pleads for them (Rom. 8:26-27). The Spirit clues believers in on the "hidden wisdom of God" (1 Cor. 2:7), which the present age cannot understand, and "fathoms everything, even the depths of God" (1 Cor. 2:10). The Spirit teaches (1 Cor. 2:13), gives gifts, and helps believers understand the gifts (1 Cor. 2:12, 14). The Holy Spirit coordinates with believers' spirits and thereby inspires their willing and knowing (Gal. 4:6; Rom. 8:15). Paul's affirmation of the Spirit's power to instruct on matters of moral reckoning is nowhere clearer than in his counsels to the Corinthians regarding divorce (1 Cor. 7:10-16). Paul thinks that widows would do better not to remarry even though they are free to do so. (On this issue, as on others in this section of his letter, Paul is heavily influenced by his conviction that the end of the age is at hand; 1 Cor. 7:8-9, 39-40.) As if to authenticate his judgment further Paul declares: "I think that I have the Spirit of God" (1 Cor. 7:40 RSV). In effect, Paul reminds the Corinthians that his moral counsel is assisted by the Spirit, as is the counsel of every believer.

The corrosive power of sin destroys human powers of discernment. Whether it be through a darkened and senseless heart (Rom.

1:21) or by means of a mind that fails the test (Rom. 1:28), sin incapacitates and holds people under its sway. By God's grace, the heart is granted spiritual circumcision and thereby renewed as the proper locus of willing (Rom. 2:29) and the mind is refurbished (Rom. 12:2). When a believer's spirit, heart, and mind are revitalized he or she can depend on them to be coordinated in the discernment of God's will and proper behavior (Rom. 12:2; cf. 1:28). In the life of faith, praying with the spirit and praying with the mind must be contemporaneous and coordinated. This is true also of singing (1 Cor. 14:15) and, presumably, of all of one's life.

All believers, therefore, have primary and immediate resources for reckoning proper behavior: God's Holy Spirit working with their revitalized spirits, and their own renewed minds and hearts.

Imitation of Paul

Paul unabashedly and repeatedly offers himself as an example worthy of imitation. In his Letter to the Philippians, a community with a strong and lasting affinity for Paul, he writes: "What you have learned and received and heard and seen in me, these things do and the God of peace will be with you" (Phil. 4:9). Another example may be seen in 1 Thessalonians, where Paul, torn from the midst of this new assembly of believers, reminds them of his comportment while with them and urges them to continue making him their model (1 Thess. 1:6; 2:9-12).

Paul is a valid model because he patterns himself after Christ, because he understands the gospel and the life appropriate to it, and because his actions and comportment openly reflect God's grace.

Paul has what he calls his "ways." Paul's ways have enough fixed content that he can refer to them in letters and expect his readers to remember and recognize them (1 Cor. 7:17; 11:16; 14:33b); he also can entrust a representative to refresh a church's memory of them in his absence (1 Cor. 4:17). Paul's teaching is coordinated with his actions, so that whether his followers have learned by seeing him or by listening to him, they have a solid example to follow.

Paul often uses the first person plural when he writes. (Of course, this may be because all of the undeniably authentic Pauline letters except for Romans are authored by at least one other person.) Paul's predilection for the first person plural causes some interpretive dilemmas as to whether he thinks what he says about himself (using "we") is also true of other believers (cf. 2 Cor. 5:6-9). In some passages, Paul's "we" unambiguously points directly to himself (e.g., 2 Cor. 1:12-14). In other passages, however, Paul's plural self-references may be a rhetorical strategy by which the readers are encouraged to accommodate more fully to Paul's pattern (cf. 2 Cor. 5:14-21).

Paul's encouragements to his followers to imitate him abound (1 Cor. 11:1; Gal. 4:12; Phil. 3:17; 1 Thess. 1:6). He thinks of his followers as children in the faith whose father he has become (Philemon 10; 1 Cor. 4:14-15; 1 Thess. 2:7, 11). He expects them to become in many ways like their parent, as was usual for children in those days. With the Corinthians the appeal to imitation comes directly in the father–child context: "I appeal, therefore, to you, become imitators of me" (1 Cor. 4:16).

Christ as Pattern-Setter

The pattern that believers should follow stems in part from Christ. Although Paul never resorts to psychologizing Jesus and never urges believers to figure out what Christ might have done in a particular situation, he does see that in certain ways believers can learn proper behavior by imitating Christ. First, as Christ has welcomed all believers, so all believers must welcome one another despite their differences (Rom. 15:7). Second, the gentleness and clemency of Christ (2 Cor. 10:1) serve as a reminder to Paul that, though his walk is in this world (*en sarki*), his comportment must not be in terms of this age (*ou kata sarka;* 2 Cor. 10:3). Finally, Christ's choosing to identify with human beings rather than grasping equality with God (Phil. 2:6-7) and his obedience to God become the master pattern by which believers are to structure their lives (cf. Phil. 2:3-4, 12-13).

Imitation of Others

Paul expects followers to take special notice of the ways in which his representatives such as Timothy and Titus live. Like Paul, they offer a living witness to how one should behave. In fact, they are Paul's doubles. Timothy is like a son to Paul in his service for the gospel (Phil. 2:22); he "works the work of the Lord" just as Paul does (1 Cor. 16:10). Timothy stands out as exemplary when he shows himself "genuinely anxious concerning matters pertaining to you" (Phil. 2:20). Others, Paul says, look after matters that concern themselves instead of the things of Christ Jesus; not so Timothy (Phil. 2:21). The Philippians are expected to learn how to behave toward one another by noticing how Timothy practices his genuine concern for the well-being of others (cf. Phil. 2:3-4). Paul praises God for giving Titus "the same earnestness concerning you" (2 Cor. 8:16). Believers can look to Paul's primary representatives to learn how to keep their lives focused on the gospel and how to practice genuine concern and interest in matters that bear on others.

The circle widens as Paul sees other exemplary people emerging in the various communities. After urging imitation of himself, Paul counsels the Philippians to "keep your eyes fixed on the ones who walk just as you have an example in us" (Phil. 3:17).

Individuals such as Stephanas, Fortunatus, and Achaicus are noted as persons from whom others can learn proper comportment in the faith (1 Cor. 16:18). Philemon, by his life of exemplary love, has refreshed the saints (Philemon 7). Phoebe, known for her helpfulness, should be treated to the kind of assistance for which she is known (Rom. 16:1-2). Epaphroditus was so devoted to the work of Christ that he drew well-nigh to death and thus exemplifies the proper way to focus one's life (Phil. 2:29-30). Paul tells the Philippians to honor all people who practice their faith in this way (2:29). Even though Euodia and Syntyche are in some difficulty at the time of Paul's writing, he nevertheless portrays them as capable of emulation in other particulars (Phil. 4:3).

Unnamed people or groups also serve as models. "Recognize the ones who labor among you and who show concern for you in the Lord and who admonish you; esteem them beyond all bounds in love on account of their work" (1 Thess. 5:12-13). By that description Paul highlights many of faith's purposes. The brother who is "esteemed in the gospel throughout all the churches" is apparently so well known by the Corinthians that Paul does not need to name him (2 Cor. 8:18-19). People dubbed by Paul as fellow workers and laborers should be granted leadership status (1 Cor. 16:16). In the Pauline churches leaders emerge because of their work and service in the gospel. Others are urged to look to them for patterns of behavior.

Households and churches may also serve as pattern-setters. Stephanas's entire household is exemplary of service to the saints

(1 Cor. 16:15). The Thessalonian church is a *typos*, an example, to all the Macedonian and Achaian believers (1 Thess. 1:7) so that Paul does not have to say anything because "the word of the Lord sounded forth" from them (1 Thess. 1:8). Their collective life effectively and powerfully reflects the gospel (1 Thess. 1:9-10). The Corinthians' zealous first response to the collection appeal was offered by Paul to the Macedonians as a pattern (2 Cor. 9:2). To encourage emulation, Paul in turn tells the Corinthians of the Macedonians' eagerness and performance with respect to the collection (2 Cor. 8:1-2).

What Believers Know

When faced with a problem in one of his churches or when asked for moral counsel, Paul's basic procedure is to ask what all believers should know, rehearse it, and then reason from it. In the following sections we will examine this fundamental Pauline moral pattern under the categories of scripture, other traditions, and maxims.

Paul's Moral Pattern

The Corinthian converts have some contact with cults and their adherents, and the practical issue of whether believers can eat meat offered in service to a cult deity has arisen (1 Cor. 8:1). In his response, Paul first rehearses what some believers know: "no idol exists in the world" and "there is no God but one" (1 Cor. 8:4). Then the reasoning unfolds in two directions: the one ascribes all things' existence to the sole God (8:6); the other wrestles with how that knowledge should be used as one lives with others who do not know that there is only one God (8:7-13).

Another, perhaps less obvious example of Paul's fundamental moral pattern comes in response to matters of human sexuality and marriage raised by the Corinthians. In the middle of a discussion of various concerns about sexuality and without any "we know" formula, Paul suddenly introduces rhetorically balanced reflections about circumcision and uncircumcision (1 Cor. 7:17-20) and slaves and free people (7:21-24). These reflections are framed by three admonitions that each person should live the life of faith in the place where he or she was called (7:17, 20, 24). The Corinthians have been taught the same pre-Pauline tradition that is reflected in Gal. 3:28: "There is neither Jew nor Greek, there is neither slave nor free, there is neither male nor female; for you are all one in

Christ Jesus" (RSV; cf. 1 Cor. 12:13). Paul reasons from what is known about Jews and Greeks, about slaves and free people, to construct what human sexuality and marriage would be like between persons who "are all one in Christ Jesus." Paul concludes: "The wife does not rule over her own body, but the husband does; likewise the husband does not rule over his own body, but the wife does" (1 Cor. 7:4 RSV). The same evenhandedness is reflected in Paul's counsel concerning anxiety (7:32-35): he shows equal concern for men and women as he encourages them to maximize their devotion to the Lord. Paul looks at human relations in light of what all believers know, namely, that they have equality in Christ (cf. Gal. 3:28), and then tries to do moral reckoning.

Knowledge from Scripture

Scripture functions in a wide range of ways in Paul's moral reckoning. It provides examples by which believers should be guided. Abraham, in his trusting dependence, is a classic type for Paul. Persons who trust and give glory to God as Abraham did, whether they be Jews or gentiles, become Abraham's children, children of the promise (Rom. 4:16). Further, whatever one makes of the events reported in scripture, such as the wilderness wanderings (1 Cor. 10:1-5), Paul claims they "were written down for our instruction, upon whom the end of the ages has come" (1 Cor. 10:11 RSV). Those ancient wanderers engaged in immorality (*eporneusan*) and were struck down. They tested God; they grumbled and were destroyed (10:8-10). Paul thinks that believers ought to learn from those forebears who, although they were baptized and ate and drank the spiritual food (10:1-5), were not insulated against God's displeasure and judgment. *Porneia* brought about rejection in their time just as in Paul's time.

Scripture gives insight into the nature of things. For example, scripture testifies to human proclivity for sin (Rom. 3:10-18). Scripture also declares that "the earth is the Lord's and the fullness thereof" (1 Cor. 10:26; Ps. 24:1), and thereby justifies Paul's argument that a believer can eat whatever is sold in the meat market (1 Cor. 10:25).

Paul sees strong endorsement in the law for the centrality of love in human relations. All the commandments are epitomized in Lev. 19:18: "You shall love your neighbor as yourself." The fullness of the law is love (Rom. 13:8; cf. Gal. 5:14). Faith expressing itself in love, as it is supposed to (Gal. 5:6), confirms or validates (*histēmi*) the law (Rom. 3:31) because love is "the work of the law," what the law requires (Rom. 2:15; cf. 2:26, 8:4).

Scripture also provides Paul with guidelines for the conduct of affairs within the community. When he anticipates a personal confrontation with his Corinthian opponents, he cites a biblical text as the evidential norm by which he will operate when he arrives in Corinth: "Every word shall be confirmed by the mouth of two or three witnesses" (2 Cor. 13:1; cf. Deut. 19:15).

Paul sees principles that apply to his churches in descriptions of past events and practices. The scripture "He who gathered much had nothing over, and he who gathered little had no lack" (2 Cor. 8:15 RSV; cf. Exod. 16:18) provides the guideline by which he encourages those in abundance to share with those in need.

References to scripture are weighty in Paul's view and he assumes that his gentile converts will grant them authority. Scripture is, therefore, a significant part of what he and his followers know and are expected to acknowledge. Most of Paul's churches were composed predominantly of gentiles, so it is not surprising that scripture often was not Paul's first recourse for moral deliberation; however, he clearly expects gentiles to honor scripture's authority and guidance (cf. 1 Cor. 10:6-11; Rom. 15:4; 1 Cor. 9:10).

Paul's references to scripture in matters of moral reasoning often seem to play a confirming, rather than initiating, role; that is, Paul uses scripture to support a position at which he may have arrived by other means. But this is very difficult to assess with any certainty because the scriptures were so much and so fully a part of his thought world.

Knowledge from Other Traditions

Traditions derived from believers prior to and contemporary with Paul also play a significant role in his thought world. We have already noted the way in which the pre-Pauline baptismal tradition reflected in Gal. 3:28 functioned in Paul's counsels about marriage and human sexuality. We learn of Paul's teaching about the Lord's supper only because the Corinthians are, in Paul's view, abusing it (1 Cor. 11:21-22). He thinks that some of the Corinthians are taking part in the supper unworthily and calls for individual self-examination (*dokimazetō*) so that actions can be changed and judgment avoided (1 Cor. 11:27-34). To encourage that self-assessment and provide a basis for appropriate action, Paul rehearses what believers know, that is, what he "received from the Lord" and delivered to them (1 Cor. 11:23). Paul concludes his pastoral counsel with some very practical suggestions aimed at alleviating the problems of relationships within the community of faith: wait for one another and eat at home (1 Cor. 11:33-34).

Philippians 2, one of the loftiest passages in Paul's letters, is composed around the pre-Pauline hymn of Christ. Paul sees implications for behavior in the hymn's portrayal of Christ: as Christ exchanged his lofty position for one of servitude, so believers can focus on the matters relating to others; as Christ was obedient even unto death, so believers should continue to be obedient.

Knowledge from Maxims

Paul considered himself a teacher who deserved the attention of his followers. Acknowledging that he has no "injunction of the Lord" on a particular issue, Paul offers his own opinion as "one who by the Lord's mercy is trustworthy" (*pistos;* 1 Cor. 7:25 RSV; cf. Rom. 2:16). Paul is more than a guide; his role is that of parent who must pass on the proper understanding and bring all the children to maturity (1 Cor. 4:15). Paul has been the primary source for what his followers know. He has exposed them to the scriptures and to other traditions cherished by believers. He has taught them his ways (1 Cor. 4:17).

Paul's letters contain numerous maxims that play a fundamental role in his ethical reflections. Rhetoricians in Paul's era believed they could add greatly to their ethos and stature by crafting pithy maxims (called *sententiae* by the Romans, *gnōmai* by the Greeks) that epitomized and recapitulated their wisdom and teachings. These maxims and gnomic sayings reflected fundamental truths and axiomatic principles by which people's identities were defined and grounded. As one classical rhetorician characterized maxims: "Such utterances resemble the decrees or resolutions of public bodies" (Quintilian 8.5.3, Loeb Classical Library). Although the application of maxims to particular situations in life may be subject to argument, the maxims themselves are indisputable.

Paul is responsible for maxims being a primary mode of instruction and reflection within the communities of the faithful. It is sometimes difficult to know whether maxims and gnomes in Paul's letters are his creations or whether they have been coopted from his followers—or even from his opponents. In any case, Paul is so committed to the use of maxims that it is not unreasonable to suppose that his followers imitated him by crafting their own. Whether or not Paul actually composed a particular maxim, we can assume that he uses it as a point from which to reckon a moral course.

In the Pauline thought world, maxims function like beacons by which a person can navigate and avoid disaster. Because of maxims' general nature, the same maxim can be used in various situations. On several occasions Paul uses a single maxim for moral leverage in very different circumstances. "There is no God but one" (1 Cor. 8:4) provides the vantage point from which Paul sorts through believers' relationships to the mystery cults (1 Corinthians 8) and also helps one keep perspective on the proper place of the law in one's life (Gal. 3:19-20). The maxim "God is not a God of disorder but of peace" (1 Cor. 14:33) provides a warrant for the call for orderliness in the Corinthian worship services and the justification for divorce when an unbelieving partner wants to dissolve a marriage (1 Cor. 7:15). Likewise, the pre-Pauline tradition that is abbreviated and recast as a maxim in various ways—"Neither male nor female, neither Jew nor Greek, neither slave nor free"—functions, as we have seen, in one context as a fulcrum for reckoning the proper relationships between males and females (1 Corinthians 7) and in another place as a way of understanding how people can retain their differences and yet have unity in Christ (1 Cor. 12:12-13).

At times Paul employs maxims as the capstone of an argument. In these instances, the maxim stands in a place of great rhetorical emphasis, at the end, suggesting that the principle enunciated here is foundational to the claims that have preceded it. For example, when Paul deals with his Corinthian opponents and appears to be drawn into the very comparison and contention that he finds so distasteful, he seems to regain his posture as he moves toward the maxim that pulls one phase of the argument to a close: "For not the one commending himself but the one whom the Lord commends— that one is tried and true" (2 Cor. 10:18; cf. 1 Cor. 14:33). In the maxim Paul acknowledges that self-commendation has no weight or merit when compared with the Lord's commendation.

For Paul, maxims not only conclude arguments, they sometimes launch them. Maxims can be the touchstone from which one tests out options. The claim that "there is no idol in the world" (1 Cor.

8:4) provides the starting point from which Paul and his followers can sort through what is involved in eating food that has been offered to idols (1 Cor. 8:4-13).

In all these examples, Paul expects that all will assent to the truth of the maxims. The maxims reflect the very foundation of the faithful community's being, their common point of cohesion. So the maxims become points of agreement from which one may try, through application, to discern proper behavior.

Paul sometimes stacks maxims one upon another, usually in the latter portions of a letter and often with no discernible link from one to the next. In these instances they stand as snapshots or vignettes of the proper life. "Bless the persecutors, bless and do not curse" (Rom. 12:14). "Repay no one evil for evil; have regard for good before every one; if it is possible, in matters bearing on you, be peaceful with all people" (Rom. 12:17-18). "See that no one repays evil for evil, but always pursue the good for one another and for all; always rejoice; constantly pray" (1 Thess. 5:15-16).

Because maxims enhanced the authority and prestige of the one who employed them, it is not surprising that Paul stacks them at crucial places in his letters, in part at least to commend his authority. In Romans, for example, the stack (Rom. 12:9-21) comes just after his call for all the diversity of believers to be placed in service of the community, and prior to his treatment of love (Romans 13) and differences of opinion and practice within the community (Romans 14 – 15). In the letter fragment in 2 Corinthians 10 – 13 the maxim stack comes at the very end, as a final affirmation of Paul's authority and a last appeal for unity and peace (2 Cor. 13:11-13). A series of maxims also occurs near the end of 1 Thessalonians (5:12-22).

Though a modern reader cannot discern an obvious connection between every maxim and the situation that prompted Paul to write the letter, quite frequently one can see a connection. For example, the repeated concern in Romans with judgment among believers might provide a link to the maxim material about avenging oneself on enemies (Rom. 12:19-20). One might also see a connection between the divisive Corinthians and the maxims regarding agreement with one another and living in peace (2 Cor. 13:11). Similarly, admonitions to "encourage the fainthearted" and "help the weak" and "have patience" are appropriate to the beleaguered situation of the youthful church represented in 1 Thessalonians.

Any modern efforts to see connections between the maxims and the situations lack the immediacy that the first readers and hearers of the letters must have had, given their detailed knowledge of their own situation and, with the exception of Romans, their intimate knowledge of Paul and his teachings. We can, however, touch on the nature and function of maxims in Paul's letters and in his teaching. Maxims, by their general nature, call for involvement and self-application. They invite the reader or hearer to engage them, to try them on to see how life would look if one lived in accord with them. How, for example, would one "triumph over evil in the good" (Rom. 12:21)? What would be entailed in holding on to the good and keeping distance from every form of evil (1 Thess. 5:21-22)? Such moral counsel resembles guidelines more than casuistry, and goals more than particular steps along the way.

Maxims as a mode of moral counsel fit Paul's thought world. They are a good teaching device in that they do not simply prescribe particular forms love should take, but leave it up to the determination of the individual. They demand direct and active participation and provide the individual with a resource that in some future situation may yield an insight into how to live in faithfulness before God. Maxims steadfastly keep the responsibility for direction squarely upon the believer—just as Paul, eschewing command, did with Philemon—who must determine what light refracts from that maxim onto his or her own situation.

Maxims also fit Paul's ethical stance. We have seen that in Paul's thinking a particular action might be appropriate for one believer and not for another, depending on the measure of faith and the impact of the action on others. The Pauline maxims do not prescribe specific actions that all believers must perform in lock step; rather, they tell believers how they ought to behave with one another ("Rejoice with those who are rejoicing" [Rom. 12:15]), what they ought to aim for in their life ("Cleave to the good" [Rom. 12:9]), or what they know ("Vengeance belongs to God" [Rom. 12:19-20]; "There is no God except one" [1 Cor. 8:4]; "All things are permissible" [1 Cor. 6:12; 10:23]).

Maxims refocus the readers' attention upon the basics and reclaim what Paul hopes is common ground between him and the readers. Maxims anchor Paul's thought world and tie his followers into it.

As helpful and as powerful as maxims are, however, they are reductionist in nature. Pithy as they are, they sometimes reduce complicated issues to simple propositional form, much as modern-day bumper stickers do. Consider, for example, "All things are permissible" (1 Cor. 6:12; 10:23). Paul never rejects this claim; he qualifies it by making additions to it, so it must contain a fundamental truth for him. From what we have seen we can understand what truth it had for Paul and fill in the rest of the picture: all things are permissible *so long as they are appropriate to one's measure of faith and so long as they do not cause harm to another for whom Christ died.* Because each believer is responsible for her or his measure of faith and for living by that faith, and because each believer is responsible for the neighbor, believers can affirm the aphorism "all things are permissible." Faithful people are supposed to know the rest of the picture. Some of the Corinthians remembered the maxim but forgot the larger picture that the maxim was intended to elicit.

So as good a teaching device as the maxims are and as directly as they fit the way Paul's thought world works, they are not flawless in the way they function. Nevertheless, the Pauline maxims form part of what believers are expected to know and from which they can reflect and make their judgments about the moral life, the behavior appropriate to their individuated measures of faith.

Other Sources of Knowledge

Jesus' Teachings

Sayings of Jesus, whether explicitly identified or not, are granted authority (cf. 1 Cor. 11:23-26). Paul rarely explicitly identifies a saying as one of Jesus' (cf. 1 Cor. 7:10). On occasion he may reflect what we recognize from the gospels as a teaching of Jesus (1 Thess. 5:2; cf. Matt. 24:43; Luke 12:39-40).

However, if one may judge from Paul's treatment of divorce, even the sayings of Jesus do not have absolute, rock-bound authority. Jesus' prohibition of divorce (1 Cor. 7:10; cf. Mark 10:2-9) is advanced by Paul as the better way, the path along which believers ought to aim to walk, but Paul's subsequent comments make it clear that he thought a believer could elect for divorce even while knowing Jesus' directions against it (1 Cor. 7:11-15). A woman's choice to divorce does not cast her out of fellowship with the other believers. One may conclude that at least in this instance Paul saw Jesus' teachings as guidelines to which one would do best to adhere, but that Paul could imagine circumstances in which a person might nevertheless seek divorce and still not be excluded from the community.

If the evidence in the letters is an accurate indication, then Paul's moral reflection did not follow a regular pattern of applying some teaching of Jesus to a problem at hand. To be sure, Jesus' teaching does play a limited and occasional role in Paul's ethical deliberation, but—as one might expect from someone who no longer considered Jesus as if the death and resurrection had not taken place (2 Cor. 5:16)—other perspectives such as life in Christ and the workings of the Spirit play a greater role.

Custom and Nature

Occasionally, Paul argues from custom or nature in his moral reckoning. Nowhere do such arguments function as a single or even primary factor in determining an appropriate response. They are always adduced alongside other, more frequently employed considerations. For example, when Paul tries to justify his counsel that, while Corinthian women may continue to pray and prophesy, they must nevertheless cover their heads, he piles up arguments to support his view. Among his arguments are those our study has led us to expect: scripture (1 Cor. 11:7, 12; cf. Gen. 1:27; 2:21-23) and the reciprocity of male and female (1 Cor. 11:11) as reflected in tradition. The arguments from custom and nature are based on the cultural practices of Paul's time, in which men's hair was worn short and women's long (11:4-5, 14-15). The same type of argument is reflected in Paul's *apologia* where, in affirming his apostolic right to support, he argues by analogy that soldiers do not serve at their own expense, shepherds get milk from the herd, and those who plant vineyards expect some produce for their labors (1 Cor. 9:7).

Paul's view of custom is ambivalent. For the most part he knows that this age and its practices are under an eschatological critique; when he thinks in this way he advocates that one relate to customary practices in an "as if not" (*hōs mē*) fashion (cf. 1 Cor. 7:29-31). When Paul finds his back to the wall he tends to pile up arguments in behalf of his case; in such circumstances he will uncritically throw in arguments based on custom.

Practices in the Churches

We cannot be certain just how much the behavior in the different Pauline churches conformed. The churches were different in so many ways, and each related to Paul on distinctive terms. While the Thessalonian church was in its infancy when 1 Thessalonians was written, the church at Philippi had been in existence a long time and its life style was very much attuned to Paul's. From the Philippians Paul accepted support over and over; from the Corinthians he steadfastly refused it. From the Thessalonians what he most wanted was to know of their survival in the faith.

As different as the churches are, Paul does occasionally note that they are all expected to follow certain practices or patterns. For example, all the churches know that every person is expected to lead the life that the Lord has granted to that individual (1 Cor. 7:17). Likewise, all the churches have the common experience of apostolic works because Paul has performed signs and wonders in their presence (2 Cor. 12:12-13). Paul expects the Corinthians to recognize that the practice of covering heads, whether or not it derived from early Jewish influence in the church, is the recognized custom in all the churches of God so they in their enthusiasm should not abandon it (1 Cor. 11:16). Beyond matters such as these, there is little evidence from which to evaluate the extent of common practices in Paul's churches, but these instances do show that Paul expects his readers to know practices and customs that prevail across the churches and to be able to reckon proper behavior by reference to them.

Paul expects his readers to have a rich set of resources from which to deliberate regarding proper moral behavior. As believers make judgments about appropriate actions, Paul assumes that they will consider not only their own individuated measures of faith, not only the distinctive situations in which they find themselves, but also the vast array of resources including scripture, other teachings, and Paul's own comportment. Paul's own actions and his own teachings, especially as they are concentrated in his maxims, are the most heavily used knowledge from which appropriate behavior is expected to be discerned.

11

Acting Out of Gratitude and Anticipation

Is there a fundamental motivation for Paul that moves a believer to do whatever deeds are done? What is the driving force in the moral life of the Pauline believer?

Doing nothing is *not* a Pauline option. Whether Paul wrote 2 Thessalonians or not, the sentiment "if a certain person does not wish to work, let that one not eat" (2 Thess. 3:10) certainly fits Paul. Paul's own actions are an example: he works with his hands whenever necessary to avoid placing a burden on anyone, and he labors incessantly on the honoring of his call.

Paul expects people, after they receive their call, to go on doing whatever they were previously doing to sustain themselves (1 Cor. 7:17-24). The Thessalonians, even while they were in some strife with their neighbors, were to have it as their ambition to live quietly, to do the things that mattered to them, and to work with their own hands (1 Thess. 4:11). Paul expects believers to continue to take care of their own needs. But beyond those basic necessities, why should one do anything? Why should one act in love toward the neighbor? Why should one take part in the collection? Why should one try to use whatever gifts one has?

Lacking in Paul's writings are some of the fundamental answers that one might expect. Guilt and the need to make up to God for past misdeeds are absent. Nowhere does Paul employ guilt or recompense to God for past wrongs as motivations to moral action. Paul's references to the past function as contrasts that illumine just what it is that one now enjoys in Christ. Apart from that, Paul seems content to forget what lies behind and press on (Phil. 3:13). For Paul, the thrall of the life of sin is so complete that one could never do recompense to God for its enormity. Grace, God's freely given, unmerited gift, alone has made possible the believer's present, new-creation situation.

Missing also as an ethical motivation in Paul's writing is the hope of future reward, of winning God's continuing favor by dint of high moral performance. In Paul's thought world, God is already favorably disposed toward human beings. God's grace now present in Jesus Christ makes that abundantly clear. Believers are now right with God; they are already children assured of the inheritance (Gal. 3:29; 4:7; Rom. 8:17).

Also missing is an appeal to motivation based on respect, honor, or admiration that might be gained from others. Whenever Paul contemplates pleasing God or pleasing people as alternatives — as he regularly does in polemical and apologetic situations — he sees them as mutually exclusive and firmly rejects any desire to please people (Gal. 1:10; 1 Thess. 2:4). When he does not cast pleasing God and pleasing people as alternatives, Paul is positive about the impact believers can have on unbelievers. In this context, Paul hopes that the believer's comportment may actually draw the unbeliever to the gospel. In fact, he lives his life to that purpose: "I myself please all people in every thing . . . in order that they may be saved" (1 Cor. 10:32-33). Pleasing others, as long as it is not opposed to pleasing God, is indirect but powerful evangelizing for Paul. Whatever else may be said, however, Paul suppresses the importance of others' judgments and exalts God's judgment. Paul is not concerned with what the Corinthians think of him (1 Cor. 4:3; 2 Cor. 13:7). The only commendation or praise that matters is God's (1 Cor. 4:5), and believers know they will receive God's praise if they stand firm in the faith (Rom. 14:4).

The Horizons of Past
and Future

Paul's frame of reference, his two horizons, provides the context within which we can see how he grounds moral motivation: he looks backward and he looks forward. When a believer considers the present in light of the past, gratitude is appropriate. Believers experience gratitude that they have been delivered, purely and simply by God's free gift, from their slavery to sin. No human boasting is appropriate here; what believers have is a gift. In this way no believer stands out as distinctive. So Paul wrote the

Corinthians: "For who accords you superior status? What do you have that you did not receive? And if you received it, why do you boast as one not receiving?" (1 Cor. 4·7).

When Paul looks toward the future he anticipates God's concluding actions — bringing this present age to its end and inaugurating God's kingdom — and the judgment at which the believers will be assessed regarding their stewardship. Once again, Paul uses himself as an example: he is a house servant of Christ and a steward of God's mysteries (1 Cor. 4:1), and trustworthiness is required of a steward (4:2). Faith itself is a gift placed in trust with each believer (1 Cor. 12:9). At the judgment the question will be whether the individual was trustworthy in the implementation of that faith lovingly into work. Believers therefore do works of love as stewards of God's gift of faith. With the social setting of the ancient household in mind, one can appreciate Paul's concern as house servant to please the Lord and receive a commendation from God (1 Thess. 4:1; 1 Cor. 4:5).

For Paul, then, the two keys to why believers do whatever they do are *gratitude* for deliverance from the power of sin and *anticipation* of the fullness of glory that will be granted when one's stewardship is certified at the judgment day. Confirmation of this may be seen in the way Paul understands works. Succinctly put, believers work because God is at work in them (1 Cor. 15:10; Phil. 2:12-13). Believers understand because they have been understood — God is the unstated one who understands in such Pauline passive constructions (1 Cor. 13:12). Likewise, believers love God because they are known by God (1 Cor. 8:3). In Paul's thought world, human action presupposes divine action. Human beings are always already responding to a gracious God; humans never initiate relationships with God. Any work they do, therefore, is always in response to God's enabling and empowering work in them. In Paul's view, boasting in one's works is appropriate because one is in reality boasting about God's work (Gal. 6:4). Once again we encounter the Pauline circle. Talking about an individual's works moves Paul to talk about God's work; discussing God's work leads him to reflect on what work might be appropriate for an individual or group in light of God's work. Either way the two are inextricably bound in Paul's thought world.

When one loves others for whom Christ died, then one has learned "to walk and to please God" (1 Thess. 4:1). When believers really understand the mercies of God that have been poured out bounteously upon them, they will "present themselves as a living sacrifice holy and pleasing to God" (Rom. 12:1).

Many other images confirm that Paul persistently viewed the life of faith as a trust whose stewardship demanded fruit in acts of love. Paul uses images of construction to comment on the work of an evangelist. The foundation is Jesus Christ; Paul may have laid the foundation but the real work is God's (1 Cor. 3:10). Others build upon it and their structures will be tested on judgment day, at which point the builders will receive a reward or not. God's work in Christ becomes the basis for and encourages human work and participation.

As Paul reflects, the image of building moves to the image of the temple and God's dwelling, but the perspective is the same. "Do you not know that you are the temple of God and that the Spirit of God dwells among you? If a certain person destroys the temple of God, God will destroy this person, for God's temple is holy, which you yourselves are" (1 Cor. 3:16-17). Paul's dual horizons are in evidence here. Believers have been made into a holy temple that is home to God's Spirit. In the future, God will render judgment. In the meantime, believers must not destroy the temple; or, to state it positively, believers have to live in such a way as to honor the temple and the Spirit dwelling there.

Paul expresses the same outlook christologically in his Letter to the Galatians. There it is Christ who dwells in Paul. Paul's life is so in accord with Christ that he knows Christ lives in him (Gal. 2:20). For him to do nothing would be unthinkable. For him to live inappropriately is inconceivable—this would deny and even abrogate God's grace. Paul avers: "I do not make invalid the grace of God" (2:21). The central issue in the moral life is whether one lives appropriately with regard to what God has done and is doing in one's life and among the faithful community. One's choices therefore reflect on one's stewardship of God's grace and either affirm or nullify that grace.

Several of these images converge when Paul first engages the Corinthian misunderstanding of the slogan "All things are permissible for me" (1 Cor. 6:12). He reflects on the purpose and meaning of life in the body (*sōma*), indeed in the body that will ultimately be resurrected (1 Cor. 6:13-14). As members of Christ, believers' bodies become one with Christ (6:17). The human options are sketched boldly by Paul: either immorality (*porneia*) or the Lord; either the Lord or a prostitute. If one is genuinely bonded to the Lord, then *porneia* is out of the question and must be shunned (6:18). One's body is the temple of the Holy Spirit, which is a gift from God (6:19). A more dramatic image is then evoked: believers do not even own themselves — they belong to another. "You are not even your own, for you were acquired for a price, so therefore glorify God in your body" (6:19-20). Believers are like slaves owned by another; they are like servants who have been transferred from one master to another (cf. 1 Cor. 7:23). The slave–servant context makes clear why believers do whatever it is that they do: because they have come under the lordship of Christ and have been given the Holy Spirit, obedience is appropriate, doing God's will is proper, and employing the gifts of the Spirit is expected.

Glorifying and Giving Thanks

Paul's summary judgment that human beings are without excuse, from the creation forward, for not having acknowledged God is focused on two test issues: Did they glorify God? Did they give thanks to God (Rom. 1:21)? Because they did neither, God was right to give them up (Rom. 1:24-28). Other things may vary from individual to individual but the sine qua non of the life of faith is glorification of God. Whatever the details of one's accomplishments, the test must be whether God has been glorified. Little surprise, therefore, that Paul's prayer at the end of the Letter to the Romans should be: "May the God of steadfastness and encouragement grant you to live in such harmony with one another, in accord with Christ Jesus, that together you may with one voice glorify the God and Father of our Lord Jesus Christ" (Rom. 15:5-6 RSV).

The day of judgment, Paul's ultimate horizon, is another factor in how believers decide to live their daily lives. As Paul sees it, that day is closer than when they first believed — indeed it is at hand (Rom. 13:11-12). Because the day is close when salvation will be granted to those who pass God's judgment, daily life, along with its choices, decisions, and deeds, is impacted. As a child strives toward being mature, or "perfect" (*teleios*, Phil. 3:12 RSV; cf. 1 Cor. 14:20), and as an adopted child relishes the anticipated inheritance (Rom. 8:17), so Paul thinks the believer should aim for salvation (Phil. 2:12).

In the most general sense, aiming for salvation involves walking appropriately from day to day (Rom. 13:13; 1 Thess. 4:9; cf. 1 Cor. 14:40). Such comportment commends itself not only to God, but also to those outside the believing community (1 Thess. 4:12). In a more individuated sense, one aims for salvation by running well, that is, by living up to one's call in the gospel.

So the anticipated day of judgment affects the way believers live. For believers, however, the judgment is not so much a wrath to be feared and avoided at any cost as it is a reality that the believer can use as a guideline for living appropriately in the present. Fear of judgment day is not a club with which Paul badgers his followers into line. In Paul's thought world the day of judgment is a fearsome prospect only for those who are conformed to this world (Rom. 2:5; 12:2; Phil. 3:18-19).

12

Living in the Present

We are in different times from those Paul faced. What we as modern people think we know and understand has altered our view of ourselves and our world. Although there are many substantial points on which we can make contact with Paul, we should also recognize certain points of distance. I will examine six points on which we as modern people may experience dissonance with Paul and then close with a comment about Paul's enduring contributions.

Eschatology

Paul was convinced that the world as he knew it was soon coming to an end. Throughout the undeniably authentic letters Paul consistently reflects his conviction that God was about to conclude history. Even his last extant letter, Romans, says, "Besides this you know what hour it is, how it is full time now for you to wake from sleep. For salvation is nearer to us now than when we first believed; the night is far gone, the day is at hand" (Rom. 13:11-12 RSV).

Paul's apocalyptic horizons frame his thought world. God's mystery that was veiled for so long has now been disclosed (Rom. 16:25-26). The creation, so long subject to decay, is now experiencing the labor pains that for Paul clearly signal the final deliverance (Rom. 8:21-22). That is why believers are so often urged to be on the watch, to be awake, and to remain sober (Rom. 13:11-13; 1 Cor. 16:13; 1 Thess. 5:6-8). Paul died thinking that the end was near.

Some nineteen centuries later, the failure of that expected end to arrive must gnaw at us as we read Paul's letters. Should modern readers of Paul, recognizing that his expectations about the end of history were not fulfilled, ignore his eschatology and expunge it from his theology as unnecessary freight? Or should modern readers make an argument like the one Paul made about the exodus: the events of history were really written down for us "upon whom the end of the ages has come" (1 Cor. 10:11 RSV)? In the former case, eschatology would be treated as an unessential appendage to Paul's thought world. In the latter interpretation, Paul's ardent expectation of the end would be transferred to our times.

Without its eschatology—that is, without its second horizon—Paul's gospel loses its power. Fundamental to Paul's proclamation is the claim that God's re-creation, the transformation of sin-riddled creation, is under way. Paul's invitation to faith is a bid to become partakers in and heirs to what God is doing. To eradicate Paul's eschatological claims relegates his letters to the status of source books for some general counsels and bits of moralism. When one loses sight of Paul's eschatological critique of this age and its values, then the values of one's own age creep back into one's thought world and become formative. One can see this process already beginning to occur in the pastoral epistles, 1 and 2 Timothy, and Titus.

It is a problem of considerable proportions to retain as full a picture of Paul's gospel as possible while recognizing that his imminent eschatology failed to materialize. If Paul's two-age apocalyptic framework were of the more typical type that was described in chapter 1 of this book—that is, of two successive but distinct ages, the latter coming into being only when the first disappeared—then one could move the transition point ahead to a later stage in history. The earlier picture

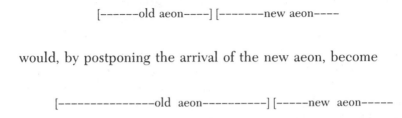

would, by postponing the arrival of the new aeon, become

The major difference would be that the old aeon would be understood to last longer before God's totally new transformation was to begin.

We have seen, however, that Paul's thought world is characterized by his strong conviction that the new age has begun in the
midst of the old age. In the death and resurrection of Christ, God
not only has signaled judgment against sin, its power, and its structures, but also has begun the new creation. The two aeons exist
alongside one another from Christ's death and resurrection until
his Parousia, judgment day. If the Parousia is delayed, Paul's
thought world experiences the greatest modification precisely in
the extension of the present. The old aeon would continue much
longer than Paul anticipated. The new aeon, still understood as
being inaugurated in Christ's death and resurrection, would continue much longer into the future than Paul expected. Even with
the delayed judgment, one could embrace Paul's admittedly rather
sketchy picture of what would happen at the termination of the old
aeon. That allows two important Pauline convictions to remain:
first, that God's ultimate judgment day and termination of this age
are still expected; and second, that the present is a time in which
the new creation continues to be formed by God. So what Paul took
to be a foreshortened present would be a very long present. The
picture as seen in Paul's letters

could be modified as follows in the twentieth and twenty-first
centuries:

Ecclesiology

Paul's ecclesiology or understanding of the church differs from our
own. Paul was accustomed to fellowships of believers that met in
members' homes (Rom. 16:5, 10, 11, 14, 15; Philemon 2). Although

he recognizes that the believers in one place belong in Christ to the believers in another place, and although he appreciates that one church can become the model or pattern for another, he does not share the view—which certainly is widespread in modern times—that these distinct churches are part of a larger entity that might be called the church. The author of Ephesians has made that conceptual connection (Eph. 1:22; 3:10, 21; cf. Col. 1:18); there the church has even taken on cosmic proportions (Eph. 3:10).

The modern reader will recognize in Paul's letters that unity in the church is not a new problem. Already in Paul's time people understood differently what was involved in being a believer. Not only are there divisions in churches such as the one in Corinth, but there are rival preachers who insinuate themselves into the Galatian churches and bid for their own followers. Paul acknowledges to the Philippians that many people preach Christ for a wide array of reasons—even to irritate Paul (Phil. 1:15-17).

As Paul sees it, one community's believers should have concern for those in another place. This is clearly evidenced by Paul's efforts in behalf of the collection for the Jerusalem saints. Paul takes delight in the Macedonians' eagerness to share (2 Cor. 8:1-4). Likewise, the Corinthians' abundance ought, in a sense of equality or fairness (*isotēs*), to take care of others' needs (2 Cor. 8:13-14). Beyond that, however, believers' connections with other believers are rather limited. They do pray for one another (2 Cor. 9:14). Those communities who support Paul in his evangelizing may see him as a link to distant believers. Agents, whether of Paul or of other churches (2 Cor. 8:18-19; Phil. 2:25-30), provide contact between distinct believing communities, as indeed do other individuals who travel for whatever reason (Rom. 16:1-4; cf. 1 Cor. 1:11).

Occasional hints suggest that Paul recognizes a nascent sense of the collectivity of his congregations. Insofar as individual churches are supposed to be swayed by practices that prevail "in all the churches" (cf. 1 Cor. 7:17; 11:16; 2 Cor. 12:13), Paul assumes some solidarity among believing communities across his mission field. Prisca and Aquila have "risked their necks" for Paul's life and been fellow workers with Paul in such a way that "all the churches of the gentiles" join together with Paul in giving thanks (Rom. 16:3-4 RSV). Also, the unnamed brother who is being sent to Corinth along with the collection is said to be "the approved one in the gospel throughout all the churches" (2 Cor. 8:18). This person has been "elected by the churches" to journey with Paul as the collection is pulled together and delivered (2 Cor. 8:19). It is noteworthy that the text does not say "church" as a collective form for the separate communities of believers, but also that this unnamed brother has been formally chosen in some way by more than one church. What a shame that we have no way of knowing what mechanisms the earliest churches had for such a selection process! At the very least, an election by more than one church does testify to a certain self-conscious cohesiveness among early Pauline churches. Those churches, nevertheless, conceive of themselves as discrete groups and apparently do not think of themselves collectively as the church; in so doing they no doubt reflect Paul's own thinking. Paul's churches are distinct communities of the end time, relatively isolated groupings of people who worship together, care for one another, and wait for the imminently expected Parousia of their Lord.

No set patterns of leadership structure emerge. Philippians alone addresses "bishops and deacons" along with the typical mention of the saints (Phil. 1:1; cf. 1 Tim. 3:1-2, 8-10; Titus 1:5-7), though we know nothing about who these people were or even whether the terms reflect titles or functions. Across the Pauline corpus, leaders seem to emerge from within the various congregations. For example, Stephanas and his household, Paul's first Achaian converts, devoted themselves to the service of the saints (1 Cor. 16:15), and Paul thinks the other Corinthians should accord those people authority (1 Cor. 16:16). Those who labor among believers giving aid and instruction are to be held in high regard "in love on account of their work" (1 Thess. 5:12-13). This fits Paul's thought world because his own authority among his followers is directly linked to his work among them in behalf of the gospel.

Governmental Structures

Modern people have little to compare with the governmental structures of Paul's time. His world was framed by the Roman Empire. He knew full well that the Roman believers, living at the center of the empire, had to deal with governing authorities, and his counsel to them was to pay taxes, respect, and honor to whomever they are due (Rom. 13:7). For whatever reasons, in his letter to the Roman believers Paul says that the authorities are servants (*diakonos,* 13:4; *leitourgoi,* 13:6) of God and that believers should be subject to them (13:1, 5).

Paul's other encounters with and statements about governmental authority should be considered along with Romans. While imprisoned, Paul preached to the praetorian guard (Phil. 1:13). He was arrested and imprisoned (2 Cor. 11:23; Phil. 1:7; Philemon 1); he was pursued by a governor but escaped by some trickery (2 Cor. 11:32-33). Paul envisions a not-too-distant time when Christ will destroy "every rule and every authority and power" (1 Cor. 15:24 RSV)—which presumably might include political authorities. The "rulers of this age" do not have any access to the "secret and hidden wisdom" of God (1 Cor. 2:6-8) or they would not have crucified Christ.

Out of such a variegated picture, how is a modern person supposed to connect with the Pauline thought world? Indeed, just where does Paul stand on his view of governing authorities? Are the authorities "ministers of God"? Or are they dupes? How does life in a modern democracy, where voting is to some degree direct participation in the direction of the government and its leadership, compare to living as one (minority) citizen in a vast and diverse empire unaccustomed to representation and sharing of power?

Social Ethics

In the letters there is no evidence that Paul ever saw the larger social implications inherent in his gospel. Instead, his focus is primarily within the believing community and how life in Christ changes and shapes relationships there. In the faith community, distinctions proper to the old age no longer prevail. Slaves and masters are brothers, even beloved brothers, in Christ (Philemon 16). Women and men have reciprocal rights in marriage (1 Corinthians 7). Jews and gentiles are Abraham's children—they are equally God's children.

Outside the church, however, there is no evidence in the letters that Paul ever expected new believers to experience a change in social identification or status. A gentile convert remained a gentile. Slaves, even after conversion, remained slaves. "Only to each as the Lord has assigned, as God has called each, thus let him walk. . . .

Was a certain person uncircumcised when he was called? Let him not be circumcised. . . . Were you a slave when called? Let it not be of concern to you" (1 Cor. 7.17, 18, 21). Three times in that passage Paul iterated what he commands "in all the churches": converts should stay in the situation in which they were called (1 Cor. 7:17). In fact, it is precisely to such a setting that Paul returns Onesimus after the latter's conversion: Paul sends him back home to his master, Philemon. Paul did allow that a slave could take advantage of an opportunity for freedom (1 Cor. 7:21), but this seems to be a concession. It is clear from Paul's letters that he believes slaves belong in his churches — and in fact Paul is attracted to the image of slavery as a proper description of human life (cf. Rom. 6:15-23) and of himself (Rom. 1:1; Phil. 1:1).

Grounding this quite conservative, even quietistic, social posture is Paul's expectation of the imminent Parousia. From his earliest extant letter to his last, Paul expected the end of this age to come very soon. This accounts for the confusion at Thessalonica when some believers died before the promised Parousia (1 Thess. 4:13-18). In Romans, Paul still expects the Parousia; there the image is the far-gone night and the impending dawn of the eschaton (Rom. 13:11-14). In the very section where Paul told the Corinthians to remain in the situations where they received their calls, he laces the eschatological thread that is the basis for his reluctance to shake up social structures: "the appointed time has grown very short. . . . The form of this world is passing away" (1 Cor. 7:29, 31 RSV).

In Paul's thought world, he and his followers stand on the brink of the end. The structures and patterns of this world, marked by sin's power, are passing away. There is no need to alter them, and certainly no need to overthrow them, as long as believers can live within them *hōs mē*, as if not, and await the structures' imminent demise. Soon the old aeon's structures and powers will disappear in the face of God's final judgment. In the meantime, believers can live the new life in certain respects within the believing community because they know that in Christ — and therefore within the church — there is neither slave nor free, neither Jew nor gentile, neither male nor female.

Paul's unrelenting focus on the end of time has a profound effect on what receives his attention. For example, Paul's counsels about marriage are centered not on how to make the most out of one's marriage, but on how to maximize devotion to God (1 Cor. 7:32-35). Long-range concerns have no importance; Paul's moral reflections respond only to those issues raised by his congregations, and whatever he engages is viewed only as a stop-gap measure between here and the imminent end of the ages. The result is that Paul's letters present a reader with a set of topics arrived at accidentally and more gaps than one might at first realize.

Anthropology

Paul assumed in his understanding of human nature that believers stood confidently before God in faith. Doubts function for Paul as cautionary signals that believers are approaching the borders of the actions that their measure of faith will allow. Where there are doubts, believers should not act. Believers experience peace and an end to the sense of being at cross purposes with oneself. Paul never questions that love can be shown in all circumstances. Believers, with their renewed minds, can know, will, and do the good. For Paul it is the person under the power of sin who is at cross purposes, who wills one thing and achieves another, and who does unwilled things (Rom. 7:17-21).

People in modern times may find these matters more complex and puzzling than Paul seems to have. Modern people may discover no arena of their lives that is not to some degree haunted by doubts, and few or no actions that cannot be subjected to second-guessing. Guilt seems ever ready to intrude. Add to this the growing modern realization of the complexity of choices — not only in the number of options, but also in the recognition that many choices rival or exclude others — and one's modern moral world is even more complicated. Many people today, noting the complex, worldwide interweaving of structures, powers, and economic interests also wrestle with the way in which one's actions or even inactions may have unforeseen and perhaps even unforeseeable consequences. In such a maze, how is one to implement the simple Pauline admonition to take care of the things that pertain to others? How are believers to love one another without causing anyone else to stumble? Currently, the most prominent, but certainly the *least* Pauline, response to these dilemmas is to internalize Paul's gospel, to reduce it to an individualistic relationship between a person and God, thus ignoring the complexity of the Pauline challenge to live out life in the world by discharging the responsibilities of one's citizenship.

Paul's Portrayal of Women

Given the cultural dispositions of the time, Paul's gospel had radical consequences for women in his churches. They prayed and prophesied along with men (1 Cor. 11:5); they were reckoned as "fellow workers" and called "ones who contend alongside" Paul in the gospel; their names were in the book of life (Phil. 4:3). They were benefactors of Paul (Rom. 16:2) and had prominence in their own churches (1 Cor. 1:11; Philemon 2).

The only place in the indisputably authentic Pauline letters where there is any question of women's full participation in the life of the community is at Corinth, a city where some of Paul's followers show a zeal and capacity to overdo at the expense of others' well-being. Honoring his conviction that individuals can and should choose not to exercise their rights when doing so might cause harm for others, Paul urges the Corinthian women to forgo the exercise of their rights. Only at Corinth is there a problem like this, and it is only here that Paul cautions the women. It is curious that some modern interpreters take Paul's adjustment of women's behavior in a single community (where he feared their exercise of freedom might abuse others) and make of it the rule by which all of today's believing women are expected to abide.

Given the evidence of the rest of the New Testament, however, the relatively open door for women in the Pauline churches did not stay open much beyond Paul's death. Later Paulinist writings such as Ephesians (cf. 5:21-33), Colossians (cf. 3:18-19), and certainly the pastoral epistles (cf. 1 Tim. 2:9-15; Titus 2:3-5; 1 Pet. 3:1-7) reflect a later retreat and an accommodation to the broader culture's practice of subordinating women.

Paul's Enduring Contributions

Individuals may have different opinions about which of Paul's many contributions endure, but two areas stand out. First, whatever cautions one may have about the perils of modernizing Paul, he more than any other writer in the New Testament struggled to identify not only what contributed most to the common good of the community of believers, but also what most benefited the individual. Not only that, Paul—again more than any other writer in the early church—weighed out the tensions that are encountered when individual and community rights clash.

Finally, of all the writers preserved for us from the early church, no one equals Paul in surveying the heights of grandeur and glory to which an individual believer may soar and the depths of self-harm to which a person may sink by self-inflicted wounds.

Epilogue

In retrospect, some matters merit comment.

First, Paul was an involved person—it was the way he thought people should live. Withdrawal and disengagement were not in his life's lexicon. Paul's theological ruminations are always lodged in situ. Accordingly, Paul has no gospel that fails to intercept flesh-and-blood life or the real happenings in peoples' lives. There is no disincarnate gospel existing somewhere that Paul has to find a way to introduce and make relevant to people's lives. The only gospel Paul knows is God's power at work in human lives and in the cosmos. As modern people, we may be tempted to distill Paul's gospel out of the particularity of letters to real people facing real runaway slaves or wrestling with sexual passion, but the distillate will not be Paul's gospel: it will more resemble ideas than the power which Paul thinks the gospel is (Rom. 1:16). The same problem faces us when we try to extract Paul's ethics from his letters. There is no such thing as Pauline ethics discrete from specific people trying to live the life of faith within the scope of the two rival ages. Put in different terms, Paul's thought world, his moral deliberations, and life in the world are so intricately intertwined as to be ultimately inseparable. That is Paul's genius.

Second, we must note that Paul's moral reasoning functions repeatedly around the categories of the "fitting" or "appropriate." The action that is "proper" is one that is reckoned in two distinct directions: (1) Is it appropriate to one's own measure of faith? and (2) Is it fitting for others who may be affected by it? Paul could tell Philemon how to respond appropriately to Onesimus, but that response would be appropriate to Paul's measure of faith and to Paul's relationship with Onesimus, and love would not be served

(Philemon 8-9). Philemon must make his own discernment of how love can properly be put to work with regard to Onesimus. To be sure, Paul, Apphia, Archippus, and the church in Archippus's house (Philemon 2) can be supportive of Philemon as he makes his discernment, but it ultimately must be Philemon's work.

Third, although Paul thinks in terms of borders or fences within which the life of faith may be fruitfully lived, he conceives of them as being there to protect, to provide safety warnings. Pauline moral borders or fences are not there to be tested. They are not there to be pushed against; they are there to guard. Apart from the vice list borders, which are immovable, the other fences established on one's measure of faith or on one's conscience or doubts are movable as one's faith grows. Some of Paul's problems with the Corinthians may in fact have come from their desire to test the fences or borders to see if they could expand them, or to see if in moving them they could affirm for themselves a greater measure of faith than they had in fact. Whereas Paul tended to regard the fences as protective warning signals, it may be that some of the Corinthians viewed the moral fences as binding and as an occasion for testing freedom in Christ.

Fourth, Paul's strong commitment to individuation among the believers must not be confused with individualism. Paul's great interest in the health and growth of the individual's faith is always set within his concern for the well-being of the community of believers, and his commitment to community is always located within his conviction that God's renewal of the entire cosmos is under way.

Fifth, in Paul's view the life of faith, when lived as it should be, requires vigorous involvement of the mind and heart. By the grace of God, believers' hearts, once darkened and hardened, become the seat of obedience (Rom. 1:21; 2:5; 6:17). Likewise, their minds, formerly disqualified because of sin, have been renewed and empowered to discern God's will (Rom. 1:28; 12:2). In Paul's thought world, believers' hearts and minds are vigorously employed and coordinated with one another as they figure out how to put their measures of faith to work in love.

Finally, it is no wonder Paul's communities had such a liveliness: each individual counted, yet the community's well-being was always valued. The community is supposed to provide a vibrant, supportive, and corrective context for the maximum development of the individual, and the individual is supposed to contribute to and care for the common good. Little wonder that the pot almost boiled over from time to time. It is a delicate balance — maximizing individual expression and development on the one hand and community well-being on the other — but its power may lie precisely in its frailty and vulnerability.

Index of Scripture Passages